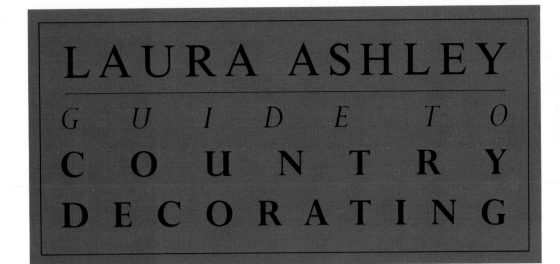

LAURA ASHLEY

GUIDE TO
COUNTRY
DECORATING

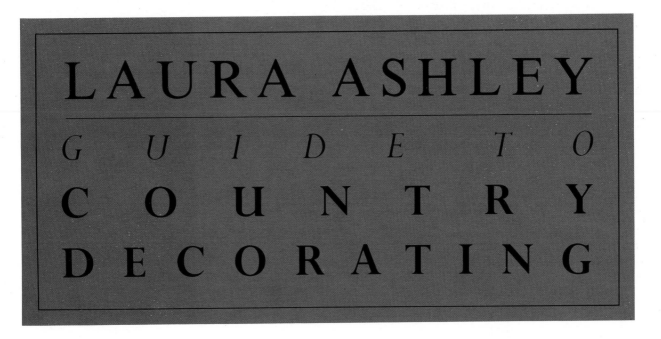

LAURA ASHLEY
GUIDE TO COUNTRY DECORATING

LORRIE MACK

LUCINDA EGERTON

JANE NEWDICK

SPECIAL
PHOTOGRAPHY BY
JAMES MERRELL

EDITED BY
ISABEL MOORE

HYPERION

NEW YORK

George Weidenfeld & Nicolson Ltd
Orion House
5 Upper St Martin's Lane
London WC2

ISBN: 0-7868-8086-4
FIRST PAPERBACK EDITION
10 9 8 7 6 5 4 3 2 1

Design and Art Direction by
ROBIN ROUT/PHOTOGRAFT
Additional design
NICK AVERY

Managing Editors
DENNY HEMMING
SUZANNAH GOUGH

Phototypeset by Keyspools Ltd,
Golborne, Lancashire
Colour separations by Newsele Litho Ltd.
Printed in Italy by Printers Srl, Trento
Bound in Italy by L.E.G.O., Vicenza

Contents

Introducing the Country Look   10

an englishman's home, cottage ties, touring provence, a taste of tuscany, mediterranean scenes, sunny swedish style, colonial heritage, shaker simplicity, the santa fé way, modern country

Designing the Country Look   38

setting the scene, kitchens and pantries, dining rooms, living rooms, bedrooms, children's rooms, bathrooms, halls, stairs, and landings, garden rooms

Creating the Country Look   94

flying finish – a round-up of techniques, country paint projects, natural bases – country floors, creating country floors, the material world, decorative details, cushions and other fabric crafts

Accessorizing the Country Look   146

a sense of nature, decorating with flowers, flower crafts, including potpourris and wreaths, festive centrepieces, country collections

Laura Ashley Shops Around the World   200

Acknowledgements   204

Index   205

Introducing the Country Look

The Spirit of the Country   11

An Englishman's Home   14

Cottage Ties   16

Touring Provence   18

A Taste of Tuscany   20

Mediterranean Scenes   22

Sunny Swedish Style   24

Colonial Heritage   26

Shaker Simplicity   28

The Santa Fé Way   30

Modern Country   32

The Spirit of the Country

At a time when it is easy to feel trampled by the relentless march of technology, and ruled by the unforgiving demands of commerce, many people seem to long for a slower, happier, more civilized life – a life in the country. Bound up inextricably with nature, the elements, and the earth, country homes – and the lives that are lived in them – share certain basic characteristics whatever their size, their value, or their location.

ESSENTIAL ELEMENTS

Above all, country style is honest, uncontrived, and unpretentious; no element has been chosen because it's trendy, expensive, rare, or old. Rooms are never 'done' in a single period or style, since they have evolved slowly, and their layered, eclectic look has been influenced more by the demands of rural life than the vagaries of fashion. Warm, friendly, and welcoming, country homes are also supremely practical, since their owners – no matter how well-heeled – are likely to live very close to the land, so every surface has to be hardwearing and easy to clean. (A typical assortment of domestic animals, or even one large hairy dog, in residence makes these qualities even more vital.) Fundamentally, a country home is never a grand formal showpiece; its timeless appearance is not an end in itself, but a byproduct of its main role as a comfortable, efficient, and appealing background to busy lives.

Above Tiny bunches of cut blooms and a spindly pelargonium link this sunny windowsill with the garden beyond.

Left A sheltered doorway is the perfect spot from which to view the leafy acres on the other side of the picket fence.

SPIRIT OF PLACE

In rural settings, the boundaries between inside and out are blurred; on warm days, doors and windows are left open so that rooms can fill with sunlight and the scents of the garden. All year round, this link is reinforced by architectural details and furnishings made of natural materials that, wherever possible, are of local origin: indigenous timber hewn into simple panelling or solidly crafted furniture, stone quarried to make a hall or kitchen floor, slate fashioned into a durable work surface, wool woven into thick, warm fabric for soft furnishings and bedlinen.

Apart from their appearance, these – along with other typical country materials like crisp cottons and linens, rough brick, knobbly rush matting, smooth, shiny tiles, and undulating plaster – contribute the dramatically contrasting natural textures that are so much a part of real country style.

Colours, too, are natural, so an overdose of brilliant primaries, garish day-glo tints, or sophisticated shades of sludge has no place in most country schemes; the authentic pastoral palette is based around creams, gentle whites, subtle earth tones, and tender pastels, blended with smaller amounts of leaf and pine greens, the blues of sky and water, and the bright, cheerful hues of wild flowers.

When it comes to decorative accessories, there are flowers everywhere; never exotic tropical specimens, but seasonal varieties fresh (or dried) from the garden, the meadow, or the hedgerow, massed artlessly in a jug or a plain vase, not 'arranged' in a highly decorated container. Treasured objects on display are unlikely to be sophisticated china figurines or exquisite silver boxes, but products of traditional local crafts such as basket-weaving, pottery, carving – or simply displayed collections of cones, polished pebbles, or branches covered in fiery autumn leaves.

SEASONAL SIGNS

Apart from the odd occurrence of freak weather, the lives of city dwellers are largely unaffected by the changing

seasons, while a rural existence alters dramatically from summer to winter. To provide heat on blustery days, an open fire crackles and blazes; not far away, a cavernous basket holds a pile of thick fragrant logs, cut on nearby woodlands, chopped into manageable lengths, and carefully dried. At the windows (and frequently the doors as well), thick curtains hang to the floor from stout poles, their design eschewing fussy pelmets, swags, tassels, and fringes in favour of the straightforward capacity to keep out bone-chilling draughts. Similarly, hard floors are covered with heavy rugs for insulation, and large deep sofas and chairs draped with cosy, comforting throws or shawls.

When balmy days return, houses, like their owners, shed their layers of warm padding, rooms are opened up to allow fresh air to flow through, and the outdoors once again becomes an extension of the living areas inside.

THE HAND OF TIME
In the past, money was often scarce for many of those who lived off the land, and household items were frequently hand made rather than store bought; these tasks were traditionally undertaken during the long dark winter evenings before television existed to provide diversion. As a result, the products of a wide range of domestic handicrafts learned in childhood — candlemaking, crochet, patchwork, quilting, rug hooking, and so on — are a typical feature of many country rooms. Because husbanding precious resources was an intrinsic part of rural life for those of modest means, these items often contained recycled materials; patchwork quilts and hooked rugs, for example, were never assembled from brand-new remnants bought for the purpose, but from carefully salvaged, often subtly faded, bits of worn-out

Above As well as heating the kitchen, country fireplaces are often used for cooking food or keeping it warm. Here, three saucepans and a kettle make full use of a white-hot blaze.

Top Fitted covers of homely black-and-white ticking will give a fresh country look to formal period sofas and chairs.

Left This rustic cottage entrance hall provides a sympathetic display area for a collection of ceramics that includes everything from dainty Victorian cups and jugs to simple white porcelain bowls and chunky modern pieces intended for display as well as use.

clothing and linen that eventually became an informal family history in textile form.

Home decorating, too, had a hand-crafted look about it; perhaps the most common of all country wall finishes is a haphazardly applied wash of colour, renewed annually in the spring. In some traditions, this was embellished with simple borders or motifs, applied freehand, or with a hand-cut stencil. In the same way, painted floorboards, or individual tiles carefully laid, were clear evidence of human handiwork rather than mass production.

Almost all country kitchens, historical or contemporary, are adorned with the end results of endless bottling and preserving. On every available shelf and surface, fruit and vegetables, pickles, jams, and chutneys make it possible for garden produce to be enjoyed all year round.

DREAMS AND DESIGNS
The fantasy of rural life is a powerful one, and when we are weaving it at the end of a bad day, it's easy to forget that, in reality, such an existence often entails inconvenience, discomfort, and adversity — in any case, most of us are tied irrevocably, and on the whole willingly, to a city, a town, or a suburb. Taking inspiration from the rustic idyll in the design of our rooms, therefore, is the ideal way to recreate the peace and pleasures of the countryside without suffering any of its hardships.

Within the broad definition of country style, there are a wide range of national and local variations; the following section covers the most influential and the most popular, describing, in each case, the spirit of the style, its roots and its main visual characteristics. In most instances, the skills necessary to recreate these looks in your own home are simple, practical, and entirely achievable.

The owners of an English country house, as opposed to a cottage, have usually achieved some degree of prosperity – they're either landed aristocrats in their manor, or agricultural landowners in their farmhouse. They may have small houses, flats or apartments in the city for convenience, but their lives and their work are firmly based in a rural environment. (This situation differs from that in places like France, Italy, and the United States, where country properties are now used mainly for holidays and weekends.)

Inside a typical English country house, the walls are painted, plainly panelled, or hung with paper of a suitable design (simple flowers or stripes, not gilded blooms, exotic scenes, or bright, graphic shapes); in the main, public rooms, the patterns might be quite large, while those in the bedrooms are scaled down appropriately.

Floors are made from timber, stone, brick, or unglazed tiles; left bare in areas of heavy wear like kitchens and entrances, these surfaces are covered with large rugs (often oriental) in living, dining, and bedrooms, where

Above Set into the recessed gothic window of this formal bedroom, a vast copper bath stands ready for morning ablutions. Wall-fixed brass taps positioned in the centre are a practical choice since they free both ends of the bath for use and are easy to reach from either one. On the bed, a simply figured white coverlet allows the rich gilding and opulent drapery to dominate.

Right Most country houses were built before the advent of separate bathrooms, so bedrooms were commonly converted for this purpose. As a result, they are often large, with imposing architectural features and decorating schemes similar to those in more public areas. Here, rich colours, thick velvet curtains, and dark timbers ensure that the mood is luxurious rather than clinical.

An Englishman's Home

comfort and warmth are important. Another characteristic floor covering is close-fitted coir matting, again with rugs or carpets on top.

Designed to admit spectacular views of the surrounding countryside, windows are likely to be large, and this size, coupled with the harsh winter climate, makes the insulating capacity of their curtains particularly important. To achieve the right body, these should be lined, then interlined, using a thick soft material called bump; to eliminate draughts and add an authentic touch at the same time, cut your curtains longer than necessary so their hems drape softly onto the floor.

Soft furnishings are more likely to be made in cotton, linen, or wool than fancy silk or brocade. The fabric we now associate most strongly with the country house look is, of course, chintz, but only in the last few decades has it been popular for main rooms; since the seventeenth century, though, when hand-printed versions were first imported from India, this flowery material has been a fixture in country-house bedrooms. Today's cheerful and widely available chintzes are hard to resist, but they should be used

individually and sparingly, never obsessively coordinated, flung over every window, sofa, and table, or tacked on in the form of extraneous borders, piping, and frills; this fussy design idiom may be indigenous to the interior designer's showroom, but you'll seldom find it in a genuine English country house.

The strong comfortable furniture is a blend of family heirlooms and newer items made by local craftsmen. Rooms tend to be large, so tables, chairs, and sofas are made on a similar scale, and tiny, delicate pieces have no place.

Upholstered seating should be generous and over-stuffed, with either fitted covers of worn leather, or loose ones made from hardwearing fabrics such as heavy cottons or linen. Crafted from oak or mahogany rather than pine, the wooden furniture is more traditional in style than rustic, and arranged in informal groups.

Overall, the effect is a cosy, cluttered one, reinforced in every room by flowers, books, photographs, pictures, and enough exotic artefacts to suggest an intriguing family history of colonial service or travel abroad.

Right In this huge drawing room with its strong late-Victorian atmosphere, the unusual bookcase was constructed from a church screen, while the billiard table can be lowered in height and converted into a dining table that seats ten. Hanging from a plain, thick brass rail, long braided curtains pull clear to reveal an arched, almost ecclesiastical, window.

Cottage Ties

Like English country houses, English cottages are comfortable, practical, and unselfconscious. Their look is more modest, though, both in size and in materials, since this style has its roots in a much poorer way of life. Furnishings are not highly adorned, but always solid, well crafted, and functional; the rooms can be irresistibly warm and inviting, despite a faintly worn and faded air.

Cottage walls are often made from thick stone, plastered or given a matt limewash finish, but not left exposed. Very simple wooden panelling – perhaps tongue-and-groove cladding – would not be out of place. The main rooms are unlikely to be papered, but a small and simply patterned wallcovering with a pale background would look charming in a cottage bedroom. Timber beams, where they exist, should be taken back to their natural finish, never painted black. This treatment, a clumsy attempt to reproduce the darkening effect of continuously smoking fires, looks far too heavy in most cases. If stripping is not possible, consider giving your beams the same pale colour as the walls and ceiling which, unlike dead black, would highlight their rich texture.

Floors, too, are stone or wood; to be strictly authentic, timber floors should not be stripped, but painted – like the walls – with gentle creamy colours. This is because, until proprietary chemicals were invented to deal with woodworm, a painted finish was the only protection available for highly vulnerable floors and furniture. Bare boards, however, lovingly waxed and polished to a silky sheen, have a very strong appeal, and are true to the spirit, if not the letter, of country cottage style. (The same cannot be said, though, for stripped floors with an easy-care high-gloss varnish.)

Traditionally, cottage windows are small and deeply set. Simple curtains with a gathered heading are hung from a plain wooden, brass, or iron rail, which should be extended on either side of the recess so the fabric can be pulled clear, letting in maximum light. They are usually short rather than full length, but never hang at half mast between sill and floor.

Not absolutely correct, but very pretty, and again, true to the style's spirit, are curtains made from a pair of quilts, full or cot size, which hang nicely and act as efficient draught excluders; a single one that pulls to one side would fulfil the same function. Similarly, an appealing quilt can be displayed as a tablecloth, tossed over a chair to make an informal loose cover, or hung on the wall like a tapestry. (See pages 54–57 for more ideas and illustrations.)

Country-cottage fabrics have a homespun quality, and are likely to be plain in colour, or simply patterned with checks or stripes, like mattress ticking. Soft furnishings are not lavishly trimmed, but there may be plain piping on loose covers, or a lace edging on bedroom curtains.

Cottage furniture is made from cheap and available softwoods like pine, rather than highly polished walnut or mahogany. Here, too, the traditional finish is paint, perhaps embellished with hand-painted motifs but, again, the stripped and waxed look is fine. (Remember, though, that most new pine furniture has a shiny, permanent lacquer on it, so you can never achieve the soft patina that comes from years of

Above Converted into a separate cottage, the old kitchens and scullery of a late seventeenth-century manor house provide the perfect setting for a summer lunch, in a room no less charming for the faintly faded look of its peeling walls, mismatched furniture, and uneven quarry-tiled floor. The latter is a result of the tiles being laid directly onto the earth since, as was often the case, the structure has no foundations. A pair of soft old cotton curtains with their own tiny pelmet hang at the deep casement window; thoroughly English in pattern and style, these were actually discovered in a French country market.

polishing.) Lines are simple and construction is rustic; ladderback chairs with rush seats are characteristic of the style, as are three-legged tables and stools designed to remain stable on bumpy floors.

Accessories hint at use rather than pure decoration: baskets to hold logs or needlework, for example, rugs and throws for warmth, candles to provide soft, glowing light.

Right In this unpretentious cottage parlour, a sturdy oak coffer holds enough split logs to last out the coldest spell. Overhead, the dark beams are balanced by a deeply polished wooden floor; the skirting (baseboard) has been stripped to blend with this rather than painted to match the walls, thus increasing the apparent floor area. Suspended from a stout brass rail are curtains in William Morris's Strawberry Thief design.

Touring Provence

Heavily influenced by the brilliant sunshine and enveloping heat of southern France, Provençal style is elegant, but simple and rather sparse, owing less to the formal manor or the poor cottage than to the prosperous farmhouse. Indeed, a typical Provençal home is a small, stone- or clay-built farmhouse, called a *mas*, with thick walls designed to keep out the searing heat. Family life tends to centre around the kitchen, not for warmth as in less balmy climates, but because cooking and sharing meals are a central part of French country living.

The strongest expression of Provençal style is probably the use of colour; all the decorative elements compete with each other in the depth and richness of their hues, which are inspired by local flora and intensified by the strong clear light; the plain walls of the large low rooms, for example, are washed with burnished gold, rose pink, ripe apricot, buttery cream, or mellow honey. Even cool tones like lavender blue and deep violet, which could feel chilly under less intense illumination, give off a warm subtle glow.

On the floor, the most common surface is locally fired terracotta tiles, often scattered with small rugs in similar, rather than contrasting, colours. In the kitchen, ceramic tiles are typical; black and white ones laid in a classic chequerboard pattern would look authentic. A large range of tiles is manufactured in the area, so they are widely used for walls, work surfaces, and even table tops – in white or plain colours, or adorned with a simple, colourful pattern. Upstairs, where floor tiles would be too heavy to cover a large area, plain boards are laid, then left in their natural state, or given a translucent stain.

The Provençal decorating style is much less cluttered than in English country dwellings, largely because so much time is spent outside; even meals are taken *al fresco* whenever possible. Furniture is large and solid, never fussy, but always graceful with generous curves and clean lines. This look is typified by the huge and traditional *armoire*, an all-purpose cupboard that can be pressed into service in every room. These, like most other items, are made from indigenous walnut or fruitwood, appealingly carved or, in less well-off homes, hand-painted with *naïf* images, faded where they were once bright.

Below Spread thickly over the chimney breast and mantel as well as the walls of this farmhouse, a coat of typically rough plaster has been scored with large diamond motifs while it was still wet. Sitting by the fireplace is a woven armchair made from thin strips of chestnut fixed to a frame made from the same, locally grown, timber.

Perhaps the best-known feature of Provençal style is the cotton fabric woven and printed there, with its small vivid motifs copied from seventeenth-century Indian handprints. These prints have been manufactured for over 200 years in Tarascon and can be used for soft furnishings of any kind: loose covers, quilts, tablecloths (made in practical PVC-covered cotton for the kitchen), and cushions. Curtains can be made from this material as well, or from white cotton or lace, but whatever the fabric, they are hung from simple wooden rails. Shutters protect against the occasional fierce cold mistral wind.

Flowers are also an important part of Provençal style; hydrangeas, geraniums, sunflowers, and wisteria grow freely, but the quintessential flower of the region, and one of its most important exports, is lavender. Arranged in tubs, or dried and piled in baskets, this intoxicating herb will fill any room with the scent of Provence.

Above Subtly washed walls in pale terracotta make an ideal foil for the brilliant sea-blue of the painted doors and matching *armoire* in this conservatory dining room. The table itself is covered with bright cotton cloths layered in contrasting Provençal patterns, while lavender and lemons, two of the region's most important exports, provide decoration.

Above Cluttered with baskets of locally produced food and wine for supper, this cream-washed entrance hall exhibits many characteristics of Tuscan style: prodigal use of timber in the ceiling and stairway as well as the carved chest; delicately wrought iron in the baluster and candle sconces; and cool flooring of ochre-hued stone. On the wall is an elaborate fresco depicting preparations for a meal that is likely to differ very little from the one about to be served.

Left A simpler fresco, added as part of sixteenth-century renovations to a fourteenth-century fortified tower. Painted, like all frescoes, in watercolour on wet plaster, this one has a stylized design of stems, leaves, flowers, and fruit. Repeated all around a terracotta-floored bedroom, the motifs represent crops grown on the estate, and therefore symbolize its fruitfulness and wealth.

A Taste of Tuscany

Tuscany's country homes, like those of Provence, were mostly farmhouses originally, with thick stone walls and large airy rooms that stay cool despite the temperature outside. The climate is more temperate here, though, and many houses have a broad terrace that leads out onto the garden and the undulating Italian countryside beyond.

In Tuscany, too, colour is very important, but is slightly less intense, so gentler, earthier hues are more common: soft pinks, browns, and creams are typical, but the most strongly characteristic shades are warm and sun-baked, like yellow ochre and rich terracotta. Tuscan rooms have rough-plastered walls, unevenly washed with once-strong tints that have taken on a faded, almost weather-beaten look. To provide a cool surface underfoot, floors are made from brick, terracotta, or ceramic tiles, or locally quarried stone such as the distinctively blue-grey *pietra serena* (literally 'calm stone').

Despite their rustic shell, Tuscan rooms have a rather formal look, reinforced by the sparseness of the furnishings, and their arrangement – not in companionable groupings, but lined up along the walls, eighteenth century style; built-in fittings of any kind are extremely rare. Tuscany is a thickly wooded region, so there is plenty of local timber such as chestnut available for making furniture; in common with many country styles, most items are large and solid, but they are also extremely elegant, and again, slightly formal. The best pieces are left plain, then waxed, but those made of cheaper timbers are sometimes disguised with *tempera magra* (meaning simply 'thin paint'), a matt watercolour finish that has been used for hundreds of years to give everyday furniture a wash of mottled colour, or a decoration of simple flowers or idealized landscapes. This technique was originally intended to imitate intricate and expensive inlay work, but it would be ideal for cheap, modern, whitewood items, or those that have been newly stripped. As well as massive and dominant chests and tables, most Tuscan rooms house a collection of lightweight, probably chestnut, chairs, that can be carried easily to the terrace or garden when required.

To keep out the harsh sun, windows are covered with shutters or curtains; fabrics can be somewhat richer or heavier than is common in other country styles, but they tend to be plain, striped, woven with a subtle self-pattern, or embellished with hand-worked embroidery; they are unlikely to be printed with colourful, highly complex designs. Curtains, too, are sometimes slightly formal – long, perhaps, with elegant tie-backs. Window grilles are another characteristic feature, and are usually made from wrought iron, worked locally and commonly used for a variety of objects such as bedheads.

As well as being a popular colour, terracotta is also the indigenous clay of Tuscany, fired without a glaze, and made into roof as well as floor tiles. One of its best-known uses, however, is in the making of containers for flowers and plants, and a typical decoration, inside or out, would be an array of urn-shaped terracotta pots filled with bright lemon trees or fragrant bushes of thyme.

Above right Converted from a disused chapel, this huge sunny bathroom still has its original deep arched windows. Between them is a thick column of golden *travertino* marble, locally quarried, which also covers the floor, lines the walls, and provides a beautiful surround for the bath.

Right Distempered in the traditional earthy pink of Tuscany, these roughly plastered walls and ceiling flatter the warm tones of stripped beams, polished wooden furniture, and brick flooring. Simple sea-green shutters and an intricate crewel-work bedcover add touches of deep subtle colour.

Mediterranean Scenes

Like homes in many warm regions, those around the Mediterranean are designed primarily to be cool; they have the climate's signature thick stone walls, hard floors, and small windows. Apart from being influenced by the sun, though, this look is inextricably linked with the sea and the special qualities of the light it reflects. As a result, the Mediterranean colour palette differs from that of most other country styles in its vividness and contrast; it is never gentle, deep or rich, and is characterized by vast expanses of pure white set off with splashes of bright sea turquoise, raw sunshine yellow, hot geranium pink, florid sky blue, or lush pepper green.

This style has its roots not in holiday villas, but in local homes, whose furnishings are plain, natural, and sometmes even slightly crude. Living is often open-plan, with the cooking, eating, and sitting areas together in one large room, its doors and windows open to admit every breeze and blur the boundaries between inside and out. Internal openings, where they exist, frequently take the form of gently rounded Moorish arches. These graceful shapes are a legacy of the 700 years during which the Muslim Moors of north-west Africa ruled much of the land around the Mediterranean, including Spain.

Uneven plaster walls are the rule in Mediterranean rooms, but wide rough wooden planks are also common. Whatever the surface, it's likely to be white, as is the ceiling, the curtains, and sometimes the floor as well. To provide contrast, the woodwork – door and window frames as well as skirting (baseboards) – may be picked out in brilliant blue or green.

Floors are hard and cold, made from tiles, bricks, flagstones, or marble, if it's local and cheap; where required, a small rug or a square of rush matting lies on top. On exceptionally torrid days, handfuls of water may be sprinkled around to cool and moisten the parched air and to dampen down the persistent gritty dust.

Many of the deep-set windows have shutters instead of curtains; to admit attractive patterns of light, these often have a filigree design or a simple lattice pattern that would be easy to duplicate with garden trellis tacked onto a sturdy wooden frame. Curtains, where they exist, are short, not very full, and unlined, made from crisp lightweight cotton or linen, in plain colours or simple woven designs like large checks or broad, bright stripes.

Furniture is basic, sturdy, and low, since the air is coolest near the floor. Woods are heavy and dark-stained or crudely painted, never decorated with borders or motifs. Comfortable seating is likely to be provided by a large square sofa with a wooden frame and close-fitted upholstery; an ordinary divan bed with a fitted cover and a pile of cushions on top (assorted, never matched or coordinated) has the right feel. Where a hard-wearing fabric is required for covers, canvas or sailcoth are ideal. For occasional use, there may be built-in banquettes, or a motley assortment of rustic chairs and stools. Storage is provided by open shelves, homely chests, and large cupboards like simple *armoires*.

Hand-made textiles, sometimes with peasant embroidery, provide decoration in the form of bright rugs, wall-hangings, tablecloths, and cushions. Glazed tiles are popular as well, and their cheerful colours adorn work surfaces, splashbacks, and window sills as well as floors. Piles of exotic fruit and vegetables in olive-wood bowls or on brilliantly hued plates make a stunning tropical display in any room, while near the door, a collection of straw hats hung artlessly on the wall would add an authentic Mediterranean touch and offer protection against the sun at the same time.

Below To let in light and air while keeping out airborne pests, long, filmy curtains are drawn around the bed in a room whose sophisticated design is an individual interpretation of indigenous style. The skirting (baseboard) is painted to contrast with the stark white walls, as is the mid-level moulding and the architrave, and on the floor, locally woven rugs soften the feel of rough, natural boards and provide one of the room's unusually few touches of colour.

Right Unevenly plastered white walls, tiled floors, and basic, low-level seating are strong indications that this rustic corner is located in a hot climate. A small, solid-fuel stove and stacked fuel suggest cool evening breezes off a nearby sea, while jars of green olives, branches of fragrant herbs, and a pile of ripe pomegranates pinpoint the Mediterranean.

Right Again, white plaster in abundance is the dominant feature of this archetypal Mediterranean room; even the storage recess and shelf in the kitchen beyond are given the same overall treatment. Here, the other characteristic elements include the Moorish arch, the simple and uncluttered arrangement of furniture, the terracotta pots of geraniums, and the clean contrasts of colour.

Sunny Swedish Style

The style we tend to associate most strongly with Scandinavia is not one that developed slowly over the ages; in its best-known form, it was created by the Swedish painter Carl Larsson at the turn of this century. Reacting violently against the clutter and stuffiness of late-Victorian rooms, this early design guru not only decorated his own country house in a way that was dramatically different from the current fashion, he also documented every part of it in a series of pictures, then had them published in book form with the conscious intent of influencing public taste. The books sold in huge quantities, and his style became a permanent part of the design repertoire.

As well as loathing Victorian gloom for its own sake, Larsson, like most people who live in northern countries, valued sunshine because of its rarity, and he set out to make every room in his house as light and airy as possible. To accomplish this, he put solid, rustic country furniture together with contemporary pieces and elegant curly rococo antiques from the Gustavian period at the end of the eighteenth century, the heyday of Swedish design. This imaginative mix was set off against a background of pale surfaces (often made from wood because of its wide availability in the country) and fresh clear colours.

To reflect maximum light in a Swedish-style room, walls are painted soft white, grey or palest pastel blue or green. As well as smooth plaster, simple tongue-and-groove cladding is common, fixed to dado (chair rail) or picture (plate) rail height, and given a painted finish. A subtle pretty border along the skirting (baseboard) or cornice adds another authentic touch. Against one wall, or tucked in a corner, a solid-fuel stove dominates main rooms, its huge body covered with ceramic tiles that can either be plainly coloured, or patterned with floral or classical images.

Floors are made from rough boards, left in their natural state or lightly washed with paint to give a scrubbed and bleached look. On top of these, marking out traffic paths, are one of this style's most characteristic elements: distinctively narrow runners hand woven in bright stripes.

Windows are left unadorned or fitted with painted wooden shutters or white roller blinds. Another typical feature, and a very easy one to duplicate, is lengths of filmy fabric like lace or muslin, softening each window in the form of dress curtains or gathered pelmets.

Like walls and floors, furniture is left natural, painted in appropriately pale shades, or limed to look sun-bleached. Here, too, charming motifs are often

Right In a country that is dark and cold for much of the year, light from any source is highly treasured. In this cosy sitting room, the sun's watery rays are supplemented by a bright fire, a traditional oil lantern, and a cluster of candles in brass holders. Painted wood, fresh gingham chair seats, and a stripey runner add colour and cheer.

Below right More stripes, this time on a narrow cotton tablecloth whose design mirrors that of the runners beneath it. In the corner, dominating the room, is a huge tile-clad stove called a *kakelungen*; produced in great numbers at the end of the eighteenth century, these distribute heat cleanly and efficiently through a system of ducts and storage bricks.

added, either freehand or with the help of a stencil. Wood is intricately carved, even on seating, which tends to have elaborate frames and very light padding, again in contrast to the hated bulbous shapes of heavily upholstered pieces. The popularity of the rocking chair in these rooms is due to the large number of Swedish immigrants to the United States who discovered this comfortable design there, and exported it back to their homeland.

Fabrics, like those in most country settings, are crisp and light; cheerful pink and blue checks are particularly popular, not only for upholstery, but also for bed covers and hangings, tablecloths, and where necessary, curtains. Reinforce the light, delicate feeling of a Swedish country-style room with accessories such as slender white candles in brass holders, discreet touches of white lace, and prettily trailing plants.

Above This old New England house was taken apart piece by piece so that modern, unobtrusive heating and air-conditioning systems could be installed under the floor and above the ceiling respectively. To cope with extra-cold nights, the high wooden bed comes complete with a traditional feather-filled comforter.

Below The authentically colonial look of this elegant living room was achieved by adding carefully chosen features to a comparatively modern house: architectural detailing picked out in a contrasting colour, timber flooring, and eighteenth-century furnishings and accessories.

Colonial Heritage

In early days, the decorating idiom of America's settlers was strongly reminiscent of their countries of origin, particularly Britain and Germany; the famous clapboard houses of the north-east coast, for example, were inspired by the weatherboarded cottages of southern England. Slowly, however, a distinctive visual character developed from a blend of things brought from Europe with those made locally, with primitive tools, from available materials. The area around New England was the first to be widely populated, and soon after, eastern Pennsylvania and the Commonwealth of Virginia were also inhabited. The style that is typical of these areas is now often referred to as American colonial.

In comfortable colonial rooms, walls are usually off-white or buff, with the woodwork – skirting (baseboard), cornice, dado (chair), and picture (plate) rails, door and window frames – painted darker colours for contrast. Paints, originally made from vegetable pigments mixed with milk, are soft and subtle in colour; characteristic shades are grey-green, teal blue, cranberry, brick red, and mustard, all with a satiny finish. The eastern United States, like Sweden, is rich in timber, so tongue-and-groove cladding (called matchboarding) is similarly popular,

but here it is normally taken only to dado (chair) rail height, and painted to match the woodwork rather than the walls.

Floors are made from native hardwoods like maple, polished to produce a rich golden patina – a fairly sophisticated look far removed from that of rustic Mediterranean planks (and one that is easily achievable with modern parquet tiles). On top of these boards are arranged hooked, braided, or rag rugs, or their far cheaper alternative, painted canvas floor cloths.

Louvred shutters (widely popular in many American rooms) are a common window treatment, as are café curtains, hung from a rail fixed halfway up the frame to afford privacy and still admit light.

Furniture, like flooring, is made from local timbers like cherry, hickory, and elm, similarly buffed to give a deep shine. Influenced by familiar European forms, typical pieces include blanket boxes, clothes presses, food safes, and highboys for storage, as well as characteristic seating designs like camelback sofas and Windsor chairs; although English in origin, the latter soon became more closely associated with the USA since so many were manufactured there. One well-known example of colonial furniture is the

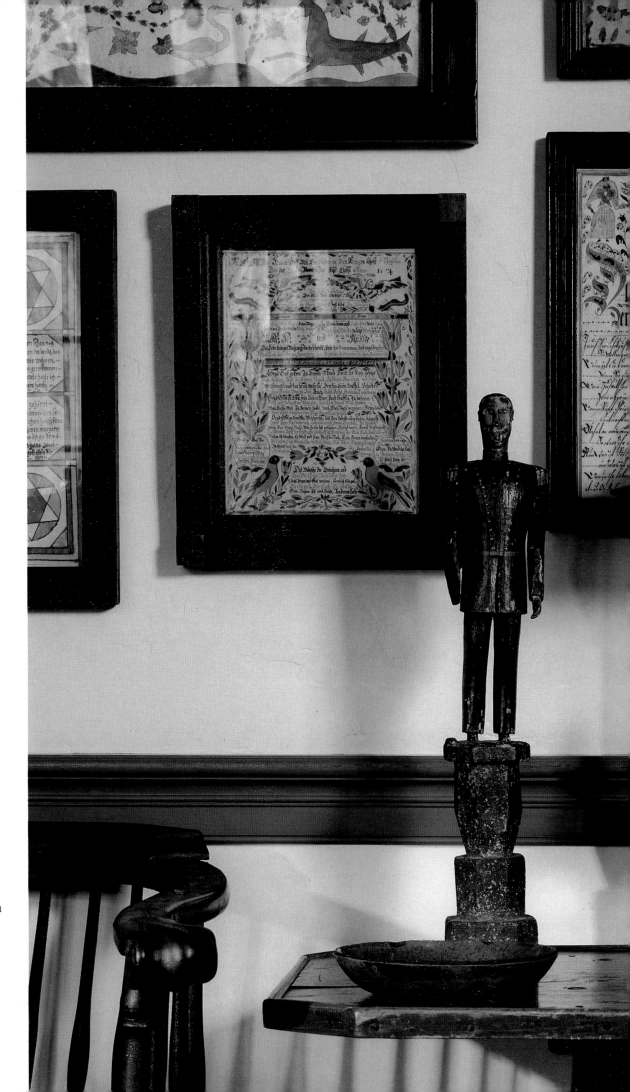

Right Very much a part of early colonial life, needlework samplers were produced by young girls learning to master the wide range of sewing skills so necessary at a time when most clothing and household linen was made at home.

rocking chair, said to have been invented in the eighteenth century by Benjamin Franklin. Another is the pencil-post bed with its high, turned supports at each corner, a scaled-down version of the grand European four-poster. Underneath one of these large beds, a small one on wheels was traditionally stored for the use of children or visitors; this was called a truckle or trundle bed.

The quintessential colonial accessory is the patchwork quilt, originally a haphazard assembly of available scraps that later became an intricate example of folk art. Another local craft, stencilling, developed out of the need for a cheap substitute for wallpaper and fabric, and went on to establish itself as a desirable ornament in its own right. Generously applied to walls and furniture, stencils were also used to give the effect of expensive rugs on the floors of poorer homes.

Decorative objects typical of American colonial style include primitive portraits, wooden decoys, metal chandeliers, dried herb or flower wreaths, and – almost synonymous with the period – needlework samplers.

Right The finger-shaped joints on Shaker oval boxes, which they call swallowtails, prevent seams from buckling because they leave room for the wood to swell and shrink with time and changing humidity. During construction, copper tacks are used instead of iron ones that would rust and discolour the wood. Finally, each box is lovingly stained with a bright solid colour that sometimes serves to identify its contents.

Left Communal rooms are usually provided with cast-iron wood-burning stoves, whose long stovepipes help to distribute warmth evenly. In the believers' dormitories, called 'retiring rooms', slabs of soapstone are heated under the stove during the evening, then placed in each bed to take the chill off the sheets.

Shaker Simplicity

The 'style' of the Shakers is solidly based on religious doctrine. A small sect that arrived in America from England in the mid-eighteenth century, they believe that every ritual of daily life is a reflection of their faith; order, cleanliness, and worship are the highest of their priorities, and one of their best-known mottos is, 'Put your hands to work and your hearts to God'. The basic tenets of their design philosophy, therefore, are simplicity, craftsmanship, and fitness for purpose. Uniformity is important as well, since Shaker society is completely communal; there is no individual ownership, and it is thought wrong for any believer to use an item that is superior to those of the other sisters and brethren. This communal way of life is responsible, too, for the fact that Shaker furniture is as light and as portable as possible so that it can be moved around as required.

Nothing is adorned unnecessarily, every detail has a reason for being there, and every object is designed with a particular purpose – and often a specific location – in mind. The resulting craftsmanship has such strength, practicality, and breathtakingly austere beauty that, 200 years on, it is still being appreciated all over the world.

The Shaker colour scheme is a simplified version of the colonial palette: walls are cream, with dark-painted woodwork and bare wooden floors, usually pine. Sparsely furnished at the best of times, these rooms look even emptier when they aren't in use, since, to give a neat appearance and leave the floor clear for cleaning, every possible item is hung on a peg-rail fixed around the walls just above shoulder height. Consisting of a length of timber inset with short pieces of dowel (very easy for a DIY enthusiast to make), this rail holds not only obvious items like hats, baskets, bags, and items of clothing, but also small pieces of furniture such as cupboards, lap-desks, mirrors (never larger than 12 × 18in to discourage vanity), and even chairs, which are hung upside down so dust doesn't collect on the seat. (Another Shaker aphorism states, 'There is no dirt in heaven'.)

Textiles are plain and homespun, woven and sewn by the sisters for both personal and domestic use. There are few soft furnishings in Shaker rooms, though, and even tablecloths are disapproved of; meals were originally eaten off wooden or pewter plates (later, plain white ones were brought in from the outside world), laid directly on a constantly scrubbed tabletop.

To ensure self-sufficiency, Shakers make as many household items as possible themselves, and virtually all their furniture. Favourite woods include butternut, cherry, maple, pine, birch, and oak. Storage units are often built-in, to make full use of the available space, and to prevent dirt from gathering on top or underneath. The internal organization of these storage pieces is impressive; each has drawers or shelves of varying sizes, again to accommodate different objects without wasting space. Often, all the compartments were labelled, so their contents could be replaced accurately, ready for the next believers who required them.

Large items like beds (traditionally single, since the Shakers believe strongly in chastity) are often on wheels for ease of movement and, of course, cleaning. Dining tables commonly have a trestle construction to allow maximum leg room, and their accompanying chairs tend to be of the ladderback type, with seats of woven cloth tape. A unique Shaker invention is the 'tilter' chair, which has an ingenious ball-and-socket mechanism set into both rear feet to keep them flat on the floor when the occupant leans back. Other characteristic Shaker items are small round-topped tables designed as candle stands, desks (sometimes double to encourage companionship in work), blanket boxes, rocking chairs, wash stands, handled baskets of pale ash, oak, and willow, and the famous round and oval storage boxes with their distinctive swallowtail joints. Although the believers use some of these boxes, many more are made especially to be sold, thus bringing in money to pay for those few supplies they are unable to provide for themselves.

Below Personal cleanliness is of primary importance to the Shakers, so most retiring rooms have their own washstand. This one, made of butternut, pine, and tiger maple, has a gently flared top and splashboard, and storage space underneath for soap and fresh towels. Privacy is afforded by means of simple white cotton curtains hung across the bottom half of the window.

Above A stone floor, small shuttered windows, and thick light walls anchor this room firmly in a hot, sunny climate. The dark, sturdy wooden bench is softened with a collection of bright cushions, hand-decorated with embroidery, needlework, and appliqué. Painted in cheerful red, the welcoming open door reflects a famous local adage, *mi casa es su casa*—my house is your house.

The Santa Fé Way

The decorating style known as Santa Fé, or sometimes Tex-Mex, is indigenous to the very opposite corner of the United States from New England, where the first Europeans put down their roots. In appearance and in atmosphere, the visual idioms are very different, and this difference is due to the dramatically contrasting influences at work. First, the cultural traditions of the south-west did not come from northern Europe and Scandinavia, but from Spain, by way of Mexico just across the border. As well as Hispanic characteristics, this rustic and coarse-textured style also absorbed those of the native Indians of both countries. In addition to this hotch-potch of cultures, the distinctive Santa Fé look reflected the region's arid climate, and the harsh life its settlers often endured.

Early homes were made from stone, or from the sun-dried brick known as adobe; inside, walls would then have been left in their natural state, or washed with white to reflect the sun, and a coat of white paint is still the usual choice in a Santa Fé setting. Floors, too, are stone, or terracotta (which resembles the original earth flooring); windows are shuttered against sun and wind, if no longer against enemy attack.

Solid, rectangular Santa Fé furniture is either dark, massive, and heavily carved in the Spanish fashion, or roughly crafted from local reddish woods, or fallen logs bleached from the sun. There is a notable absence of small delicate pieces and those covered with fussy detailing; necessary hardware like handles and hinges are made from crudely wrought iron, while chair seats are leather – plain or simply tooled. Large benches and cupboards are sometimes built-in, with capacious chests and sturdy tables and chairs punctuating otherwise sparsely furnished rooms.

Decoration, too, is on a dramatic scale, large expanses of bare floor or wall interrupted by a richly hued rug or hanging, hand woven in a Pueblo bird pattern, or with a Navajo diamond and chevron motif; bright durries or druggets from India would give the right look. Similarly designed cushions, tablecloths, or runners add further touches of earthy colour like burnt orange, brick red, donkey brown, and black. Less exotic textiles are mostly cotton, and usually dyed blue, since dye from the indigo and wood plants was easily available to the early settlers, and comparatively colour fast.

Other accessories include large terracotta pots or plates and bowls of the same material, either left natural or

Left Festooned with fiery chillies, and flanked with simple candles, this spiky cactus makes a dramatic centrepiece on a small table whose lacy white cloth gives it a faintly altar-like appearance. When they are first picked, these chillies are threaded into long strands called *ristras*, then dried in the sun until they're needed for decorative or culinary purposes.

brightly painted and lead glazed (very like modern ones from Spain and Portugal); wrought-iron candlesticks; intricately figured and pierced tinware, sometimes inset with semiprecious turquoise stones; and ceramic tiles fired with native emblems or graphic shapes.

One charming local tradition is to dry red chilli peppers, then thread them into long chains or weave them with fine wire to make scarlet wreaths, both of which provide long-lasting, inexpensive displays of colour and cheer that are extremely popular.

Right This large open cupboard, or *armario*, is roughly made and well aged, with a coarsely sanded finish that is ideal for displaying rustic Spanish glass and hand-made pottery. Similarly, cool blue-washed walls bring out all the warmth of the door's natural wood, the floor's pink-tinged stone, and the characteristically earthy tones of woven basketwork, kiln-baked terracotta, and brightly decorated earthenware.

Modern Country

Left Wide bare floorboards, crisp white shutters, and sculpted greenery in earthy terracotta pots give an unmistakably rural air to a Nantucket dining room so spare in style that it borders on the minimalist. Sympathetically utilitarian in spirit, the brushed steel chairs were originally designed for use in a French park, while the simple pine table is eighteenth-century English.

Far left Also located on the east coast of the United States, in The Hamptons, this contemporary retreat features an eclectic mix of traditional elements such as wooden beams and flooring, heirloom lamps, and bunches of garden flowers, with chunky modern seating and striking architectural details like the sleek curved fireplace with its cantilevered mantel.

Traditionally, rural styles developed along their own distinctive lines in response to local climate, landscape, and way of life. Independent of one another, they retained their individuality through lack of information about other cultures, lack of low-cost transport to carry objects from one region to another, and, often, lack of money to purchase elements from abroad even if country dwellers had been aware of and had access to them.

The look of modern country homes, however, cannot be defined in terms of colours or fabrics, since their owners can choose from a huge range of available decorating materials, techniques, and visual influences.

What's more, there is no need to adhere to a single style; if they keep in mind the basic values of honesty and fine craftsmanship, contemporary rustics can create new, exciting, and much more broadly based schemes by combining a wide range of rural traditions with the best of contemporary design and technology. If this is to be accomplished successfully, however, a few basic guidelines should be followed.

If a headily eclectic blend of furnishing styles is to be the main focus of any room, the background should be fairly neutral, with plain or subtly textured walls, unobtrusive window treatments, and unassuming floors – timber boards or coir matting, for

example, will blend happily with most things. To pull the room together visually, make sure there are some themes: a dominant colour, perhaps, or type of pattern (checks, florals etc.). Disparate styles grouped too closely together can look more like a thoughtless jumble than a skilful mix, so leave plenty of room around both furnishings and accessories.

When it comes to choosing individual pieces, the most important rule is to avoid mixing styles that are the result of very different influences. The heavy dark Spanish furniture that is so much a part of Santa Fé style, for example, would be desperately out of place teamed with a gentle English country-cottage scheme, while it could look quite dramatic surrounded by vivid Mediterranean colours; similarly, a solid square contemporary sofa would complement the bold Mediterranean look, but jar in an elegant graceful Tuscan room.

Don't be afraid to absorb technology unselfconsciously; it's much better (and infinitely more convenient) to search out a stylish television set and stereo, then leave them in plain view on a shelf or a trolley, than to disguise them behind frilly skirts, or vandalize the back of a lovely cupboard or dresser to accommodate all their complex wiring.

Making full use of modern materials and designs in an honest way is much closer to the real spirit of country style than searching out cheap (or even expensive) fakes. If you want practical, hardwearing vinyl for your floors, therefore, or tough laminate for your worktops, choose a solid colour or a simple geometric design rather than a wood-, tile-, or stone-effect pattern. In the same way, look for simple, well-designed wall lights rather than those with candle-shaped bulbs and mock dribbles of wax.

Above Only furniture with massive proportions and clean lines would suit the cavernous spaces inside these skilfully converted farm buildings. Eight enormous sash windows admit streaming sunlight into the main living and dining areas shown, which take up the original barn and the stable block next door. Above each of these is a set of bedrooms and bathrooms, and these sets are connected to each other by a raised walkway boxed in with wooden rails rescued from the old hayloft.

Right If you want to mix disparate furnishings, choose a neutral background of plain walls and coir matting. In this beamed studio, an abstracted landscape provides a burst of gold to offset chilly expanses of white and pale blue.

Remember that beautiful hand-made craft objects can be uncompromisingly contemporary as well as traditional; sleek modern pots fired in regional clay, for instance, bold, graphic textiles locally woven and dyed, or abstract forms carved from native timbers.

CHANGING PLACES

For a growing number of people, a country dwelling is neither a formal manor, a solid farmhouse, nor a modest cottage, but a completely different kind of building, originally constructed for one of a wide range of purposes, and later converted for domestic use. The recent popularity of this type of conversion is due to a combination of demand from more and more city dwellers seeking a peaceful rural existence, with the increasing availability of many beautiful and solid structures that have outlasted their usefulness.

Although these structures include windmills, lighthouses, and schools, perhaps the most common are barns and other farm buildings left unused by intensive modern farming methods and decreasing dependence on local agriculture, and churches or chapels, declared redundant by our secular society. As well as country dwellers, those who want to create a rustic atmosphere in their city homes may find the spare clean lines of an industrial conversion better suited to many country looks than the intricate and sophisticated plaster and woodwork in Georgian or Victorian rooms.

Taking on an empty, perhaps derelict, agricultural or commercial building has many advantages: endless spaces, for example, often larger than those in the grandest house; complete control over internal structure, materials, and architectural detailing; and, at the end, a home that is personal, unconventional, and unique. To get the

Above The singular shape of this towered dining room is religiously reinforced with its fittings and furnishings: the pale timber storage units and window seat have been specially made to line the wall and repeat its curve; the rosy brick floor has been laid in a pattern of concentric rings; and even the chairs at the circular dining table have been chosen for their gently rounded backs.

Right In this converted chapel, the bathroom's trefoil windows came out of a redundant country school, while the Art Deco ironmongery, wall lights, and sanitary fittings were all salvaged from a refit of the apartments in the Savoy Hotel, London.

Far right Here, a pretty blue-and-white colour theme is the unifying element in a lofty sitting room filled with simple, sturdy furniture from a wide range of periods. On the stripped floorboards, an exceptionally large rush mat subtly defines the seating area.

best from a conversion, however, be prepared to spend a considerable amount of time and money, take the trouble to find an architect experienced in, and enthusiastic about, this kind of work, and always respect the structure's integrity even if it means compromise; enormous picture windows, for instance, may admit huge amounts of light and a breathtaking view, but they'll disfigure the face of a charming old building for ever. When necessary, seek out new materials that are of local origin, or at least sympathetic to those used in a similar way nearby.

When the heavy work is done, and the rooms are ready for decorating, remember that furnishings designed for ordinary rooms may be totally unsuitable for conversions; in most cases, proportion is the prime consideration, so make sure everything you choose is on a scale to match its setting – small delicate pieces look lost in a lofty, cavernous space. Finding suitable substitutes may be easier and

cheaper than it sounds, though, since it is modestly sized items, perfect for average homes, that are most sought after, and therefore most expensive, in antique shops and auction rooms. Few purpose-built houses, flats, and apartments can accommodate the gigantic tables and massive chests that are ideal for converted properties, so these can be surprisingly inexpensive. Consider proportion, too, when choosing fabrics and accessories; a tiny floral pattern, a dainty lace border, or a collection of miniatures will be completely overwhelmed in a barn setting.

Within vast rooms, define smaller areas (for dining, working, or conversing in intimate groups) by the arrangement of furniture, rugs, and lighting. In this way, you can preserve an open, spacious feeling while creating the warm, welcoming, and infinitely user-friendly atmosphere that is the most appealing, and perhaps also the most important, quality of real country style.

Designing the Country Look

Setting the Scene   40

The Fabric of the Country   54

Kitchens and Pantries   58

Dining Rooms   66

Living Rooms   70

Bedrooms   76

Children's Rooms   82

Bathrooms   86

Halls, Stairs, and Landings   90

Garden Rooms   92

Setting the Scene

Whether you intend to create a wholesale pastoral fantasy throughout your home, or just give the faintest hint of country charm to one or two rooms, take time first to absorb some simple design tips that will help to ensure the success of your chosen schemes.

FIRM FOUNDATIONS

Before you begin any large-scale decorating project, remember that you'll get the best results if you go slowly. When you move into a new home – or even when you're faced with a problem room – never make decisions about structural work and furnishings all at once, then rush around trying to get the job finished; you're bound to make mistakes that way, and the end product could have a sterile, contrived look that is unappealing in itself and death to any kind of genuinely rustic style, which by definition is natural and unselfconscious.

Instead, do only what is absolutely necessary, perhaps slapping on a neutral coat of paint so that everything feels clean and new. Then just live in the rooms for a while, getting a feeling for their light and space, and firming up in your own mind the way you'd like them to look. When it comes to furniture and accessories, make do until you find things you really love rather than settling for second best to get the task out of the way. Almost always, the nicest rooms are those that carry on changing and adapting, as elements are altered or moved around, or new things are added.

Subtle tints　　Colour is the cheapest, and one of the most powerful, design resources available; it can affect not only the look of a room, but also its apparent size. As a general rule light rooms seem larger, darker ones smaller, but don't be a slave to this often-quoted dictum. The difference is not enormous, and it's much more important for a room to feel attractive and inviting than to appear as big as

Above When the sun is dazzling and dependable, pure white walls and woodwork are the perfect choice, especially when they're teamed with fresh blue fabrics and accessories. The seaside location of this summer retreat has provided its design theme, carried through with shell-print curtains, decorative driftwood and model ships.

Left Don't be afraid to use paint in a strong colour; it won't be overpowering if you temper it with furnishings and accessories in natural wood and stone.

possible, so if you're after a cosy look, don't worry about choosing medium or deep shades.

Another popular maxim is that ceilings should always be white to make them look higher, but again, this is hardly ever necessary, and most rooms – especially those where the walls and the ceiling meet without benefit of cornice or picture (plate) rail – will look much better and more coherent together if the same colour covers all the surfaces without interruption. If your ceiling is exceptionally low, try painting it just a shade or two lighter than the walls rather than stark white, which may detract from the warmth of your chosen style; an abrupt change of colour where wall and ceiling meet looks awkward, though, so where there is no cornice or picture (plate) rail, add a simple one yourself.

Often thought of as the quintessential country colour for walls, pure white should actually be used very carefully. In southern climates, where bright and abundant sunlight fills every room, white walls can be stunning. In more northern areas, however, where light is too often thin and scarce, or in rooms that are naturally dark because their windows are small, deep, and few (as is the case in many old cottages), stark white can easily look grey and dingy; instead, go for a richly creamy hue, a soft apricot or flesh pink, or a warm banana yellow, all of which will be much more flattering for you and your furnishings than a dead, chalky shade. Remember, too, that whitewash, the

traditional country finish, would never have achieved the pure whiteness of modern chemical paints, so a gentler hue is more authentic as well as more appealing.

Colour can do more than alter the look of a room, it can also affect its apparent temperature, and even the mood of its occupants. In a dark or north-facing room, therefore, avoid using mainly cool colours like blue, green, grey, or lavender, or team them with lots of rich cream and add polished wooden furniture, woven baskets, and a warm-coloured floor covering like biscuity rush matting. Similarly, cool colours are relaxing and warm ones stimulating, so blue would work well for a bedroom, while bright yellow is ideal for high-activity areas like kitchens. Very dramatic colour schemes are hard to endure, whatever palette they contain, so save them for halls, bathrooms, and perhaps dining rooms, where people tend not to remain for long periods.

Awkward areas   Irregularly shaped rooms, or those with sloping ceilings or odd projections, can often look cluttered even when they're empty. Here again, treating walls and ceilings differently will only accentuate the problem; to pull the room together visually, and make it look interesting instead of awkward, choose a subtly patterned wallpaper or a solid or broken paint finish, and use it everywhere.

Problem windows can be dealt with using similar visual tricks. If yours are too narrow, for example, add apparent width by extending the curtain track or rail generously on either side and allowing plenty of fullness in the fabric. To make a short window look longer, put a simple pelmet far enough above it so the bottom of the pelmet falls just below the top of the window. To cope

Above The sunny yellow walls of this Spanish-influenced *cocina* make it a cheerful place to work in at any time; as a change from white, the wooden cupboards and the wide-plank door have been picked out in a muted grey-blue that adds interest without clashing. Note the efficient organization of the cooking area, where frequently used pans and tools hang directly above the work surface so they're always within reach.

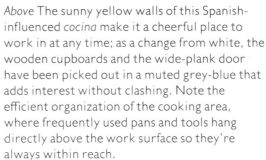

Left Design choices are greatly simplified when you search out one adaptable, fairly neutral, floor covering, and use it throughout. Here, cool tough tiles extend across the sunken dining room, over the steps, along the corridor, and into a sunny living area. To add interest, the plain tiles on the risers have been replaced with decorative hand-painted ones.

with non-matching windows side by side, fix one long rail that extends across them both, and hang a single pair of curtains.

Finally, remember that your home is not made up of separate, cut-off rooms, but of different areas that are open to each other, so make sure your chosen schemes work well together, and flow into one another without abrupt and startling changes of colour or mood. Keep this in mind particularly when

you're choosing floor coverings, since few things look uglier than completely different surfaces (or even different colours) butting up against each other at every doorway. The best plan is to choose the same flooring – or at least the same shade – throughout your home, or at least for all the rooms on a particular level. So, if the main rooms have polished wooden floors, natural cork or honey-coloured stone would be a good choice for the bathroom and

Above To disguise a convergence of awkward angles and shapes, cover ceiling and walls with the same subtle pattern, like this soft, parchment-effect paint finish. Woodwork that blends rather than contrasts, and a collection of skilfully arranged accessories, both help to draw attention away from problem areas.

Above Because its lines are simple and its proportions generous, this elegant Biedermeier sofa is well suited to a Tuscan farmhouse with brick floors and oak-beamed ceilings; a delicate Georgian piece would look lost and out of place. The iron bedstead with its graceful curves is typical of those made locally.

kitchen. An added advantage of this all-over approach is that it gives an added impression of space.

COUNTRY COUNSEL

Once you've decided on a country-inspired look, you'll need to work out not only which style you want, but also the degree to which it should be adopted so that it suits both your home and your way of life. Don't try for a grand manor-house scheme, for instance, if you live in low poky rooms

that would be far better suited to a cottagey look. In the same way, it would be folly to attempt a humble, rustic cottage scheme in a nineteenth-century town house with high ceilings and elaborate architectural detailing, or in a warehouse conversion with endless open spaces and vast picture windows; instead, create a neutral background and add subtle country touches using colour and furnishings. Similarly, try for a reasonable compromise, not only with your home, but also with your surroundings: it might feel faintly ludicrous, for example, to step straight off an ordinary suburban street, or a communal hallway, into a pastoral world complete with flagstones, shooting sticks, fishing tackle, and Wellington boots!

Whether your home is new or old, large or small, intrinsically urban or genuinely rural, there are bound to be elements of real country style that you can employ or adapt to make it more attractive, more comfortable, and perhaps even more efficient.

Wall charts One of the most basic decorating decisions to be made in any home also involves the largest single surface: the walls. If yours are newly (and skilfully) plastered, consider leaving them as they are, adding only a sheer coat of sealing medium to keep dust in and stains out. The resulting colour – an uneven, dusky, pinkish-brown – has a strong feeling of Provence or Tuscany. In addition, this solution could hardly be more ecologically sound, since it obviates the need for any kind of paint, much of which contains powerful chemicals that can harm the environment and trigger off a wide range of allergic reactions. To make a natural sealer, mix equal parts of beeswax and white spirit, and apply this with a rag, making sure the room is well ventilated. When the surface is dry, use a soft cloth to buff it to a gentle sheen.

Right A simply sprigged wallpaper looks charming in a big country-style kitchen, where it provides a perfect background for old furniture and displays of flowery china. In a tiny galley, however, that tends to get hot and full of greasy steam, a painted finish is more practical.

Right Timber cladding is fairly inexpensive, and easy for most DIY enthusiasts to install. Here, slim tongue-and-grooving (matchboarding) painted in gentle grey/green gives an unmistakably country feeling to a rather formal arrangement of pictures, books, candles and ornaments.

Above If your floorboards are in poor condition, consider giving them a coat of proprietary paint, a process that is considerably less complicated and messy than sanding and waxing. The deep blue-green colour chosen here has a distinctly early-American feeling that is reinforced by a cut-out cockerel and Shaker log basket. The posy of pink and white blooms jammed into an old metal bucket, however, is typical of artless country style the world over.

A plain painted finish is suitable for all country styles, and organic ranges often include colours that are particularly sympathetic, since they're made from natural pigments rather than chemical dyes. Walls themselves can have a matt or a silk finish, but woodwork should never look hard, so choose an eggshell paint for skirtings (baseboards) and architraves. Give newly painted wood, and even plaster, an aged, weathered look by rubbing it gently with a soft cloth while the surface is still wet; experiment first on a sample piece of wood or a hidden area of plaster, or wait until the paint is dry then go over it lightly with fine sandpaper; don't do this on paper-lined walls, though, since the edges may lift.

The recently revived fashion for paint effects has much to offer the country look, in which subtle, broken colour plays such a large part. Some of them are rather too sophisticated for true country style, but the most authentically rustic — and also the easiest to accomplish — is simple colour washing, which gives a depth and interest very like that of traditional limewash. For an instantly colour-washed effect, simply apply a base coat of emulsion paint, then water down a very slightly darker or paler shade and apply it roughly on top with a large brush, making wide, irregular strokes.

Another ideal wall covering is timber cladding in some form, from wide rough planks to the more delicate tongue and grooving (matchboarding) of Swedish and colonial rooms, either of which can be fixed to dado (chair) rail height, or above. This treatment, as well as being extremely pretty, is also thoroughly practical, since it provides efficient insulation, disguises less-than-perfect walls, and conceals awkward pipe runs in kitchens and bathrooms. Here again, timber cladding (and wooden furniture) should never be gloss painted, but given a subtle eggshell or silk finish.

If you are lucky enough to have real beams (the very idea of fake ones is an insult to the honest spirit of the country look), take the trouble to sand them back to the original, glowing, colour of the wood. The now almost passé fashion for painting them black was an unsuccessful attempt to imitate the effects of long exposure to smoke, but the result is much too harsh for most country rooms.

Floor plans   In areas of heavy wear, real country homes have a hard-wearing surface underfoot; the most common materials are stone, slate, brick, or quarry tiles, but concrete tiles will give a similar look for a fraction of the cost,

Right If stripped beams remain discoloured, bleach them. Ideally, you should use a special wood formula, but household bleach is also suitable if you dilute it 1:3 with water, then increase the concentration where necessary. Clean the bare wood with paint thinner, then leave it to dry. Now brush the bleach on generously, using medium steel wool to work it into the wood with the grain. Leave it for 2–4 minutes, wipe it off, then let it dry for 5 hours before sanding and finishing.

Right When your windows are small and deep, hang curtains from special hinged rails; during the day, instead of pushing them to each side where their gathered bulk restricts incoming light, you simply swing them out so they line the reveals. Naturally, this system is designed for short, lightweight curtains rather than long, heavy ones.

Above Country furniture is characterized by the strength of its construction and the timeless simplicity of its design; this desk, chest, and stick-back chair are Shaker-like in form, and reminiscent of an era when the quill pen and its holder were in common use.

that even proprietary paints designed for floors will wear and fade, but this only adds to the charm and authenticity of the finish. A soft-grey, limed wood floor is typical of many country styles; in Scandinavia, for example, planks were traditionally cleaned with a paste of wet sand rubbed in well, and over a number of years this treatment resulted in a typically pale, bleached look. A simpler and easier method, though, is to give bare boards a coat of clear matt varnish to which you've added a few drops of white paint. Brush this in well, leave it to dry, then seal with three coats of clear matt varnish, which will leave a soft, pearly, delicate finish. Alternatively, simply rub a little white emulsion into the grain of newly sanded wood.

In living and bedrooms, where a soft warm floor covering is required, one of the most authentic, adaptable and relatively inexpensive choices is natural coir, rush, seagrass, or sisal matting. Now available in broad widths so it can be close fitted, and rubber backed to make it comfortable to walk on and hard wearing, natural matting comes in a surprising variety of colours, from pale straw to a rich caramel that is almost dark brown. If your preference is for fitted carpet, choose one in a natural fibre and a plain, muted, colour – never patterned.

View points   The most important thing to remember about country window treatments is that they should never dominate the room – curtains or blinds are there to keep out light, afford privacy, and sometimes provide insulation, not as an excuse for extravagant draping, pleating, plaiting, and bordering, so if in doubt, keep it simple. (In the same way, cushions should be plain, or self-piped, rather than encumbered with frills, bows, and tassels.) Clearly, an English manor

especially if they are oiled or colour-washed with floor paint. For a particularly distressed look, knock them about a bit, then rub in a little dark shoe polish and finish with a coat of wax.

Wooden floorboards will suit most schemes, whether they're left in their natural state with only a layer of wax for protection, or given a coat of paint in the traditional way. Keep in mind house can take more formal window dressings than a Provençal farmhouse, but even here, simple tie backs, and perhaps a plain pelmet, will provide the right look without being fussy; give curtains a straightforward gathered or pleated heading and hang them from a wooden, brass, or iron pole – never plastic track unless it's completely hidden. Roller blinds in a solid colour are a suitable choice, but resist the temptation to add a scalloped or fringed edging, although a narrow band of cotton lace looks very pretty. Wooden venetian blinds, usually made from cedar, would suit most country rooms; frilly festoon or Austrian designs most definitely would not.

Cotton lace, either by itself or combined with heavy outer curtains, makes a charming window treatment. You can buy this material by the metre or yard in many different widths; if you lack sewing skills, choose a ready-made curtain panel at least one-and-a-half times as wide as the frame (buy two if necessary), or use lace tablecloths or even bedspreads if your window is enormous. Simply stitch curtain tape along the top and slip in the hooks. If your panels are too long, measure the excess, then fix the tape this distance from the top. When the curtains are hung, the tops will fold over to make a dainty self-pelmet.

Another popular window covering, and one that would be ideal in American, Provençal, Tuscan, or Mediterranean rooms, is plain or louvred wooden shutters. Leave these with their natural finish or paint them, either to match the walls or provide contrast.

Furnishings and fabrics   Real country furniture is solid and functional; it never looks brand-new, and whatever its period or style, it's genuine – or at least a well designed and made reproduction piece; cheap imitations have no place in a country scheme. This restriction does not, of course, include things like Shaker furniture which, although bought new, continues to be manufactured using traditional construction methods and materials. Simple in design, appropriate items will have no gilt trim, and no intricate detailing to collect dust.

Wooden furniture will vary in appearance according to the room's style, but cane chairs and tables – natural, adaptable, and lightweight – blend comfortably with any country scheme. Look for straightforward, rather than curly, shapes, and plain colours. Similar to cane and often mistaken for it, Lloyd Loom furniture is actually made from spun craft paper

Below As well as being relatively cheap and extremely attractive, coir matting, lace curtains and cane furniture can all be adapted to suit a wide range of country decorating styles. Similarly, this Mediterranean-style bedroom features plain wooden shutters that would look equally at home in a Colonial townhouse or a Provençal *mas*.

Above To give the right look, bed linen and towels in a pastoral scheme should be basically white and made from natural fibres like cotton or, for really luxurious sheets and pillowcases, linen. No longer required for their original purpose, the flower-strewn chamber pots in this pretty bathroom make a charming display with their matching ewer, basin, and lidded storage jar.

woven with paper-wrapped wire; unlike cane, this material won't split and crack, and it's even immune to woodworm attack.

The most appropriate fabrics in country rooms are made from natural, rather than man-made fibres; this not only gives them a pleasing and traditional look and feel, it also means they're biodegradable, and they contain no harmful chemicals. Like country furniture, fabrics should never look stiff, bright, and new; to give a faded appearance to cottons and linens (never delicate materials or synthetics), soak them in a solution of household bleach. Experiment first with a very weak solution, then add more until you get the effect you want, keeping a close eye on the process and rinsing well afterwards. To give a charmingly mellow look to light-coloured prints,

pale colours, and whites (including those that have gone grey), dip them in a weak solution of cold tea. This ingenious trick was widely used in the late 1940s and 50s by the brilliant and innovative interior designer Nancy Lancaster; another of her tactics was to drag sofas and chairs outside where they were aged quickly by the sun and the rain.

Finishing touches The easiest way to add rustic charm to any room is with a few well-chosen details and accessories.

Stencilling, originally a country craft intended to imitate expensive wallpaper (and sometimes used on floorboards to give the effect of a colourful carpet), can be applied to any surface: walls and floors, of course, but also furniture, fitted cupboards, and small items like wooden boxes, trays, and baskets. Use ordinary paints, car spray paints, or purpose-made sticks of colour, which are the easiest to work with, but keep colours soft and subtle, and stick to simple shapes rather than intricate and sophisticated designs featuring swags and urns.

Leafy and flowering plants will help to bring the outside in, especially if you choose large, bushy specimens, or group small ones together to make a luxuriant display. Make sure to choose those that are reasonably local in origin, though, rather than exotic species from faraway lands. To disguise an ugly urban outlook, fix rows of shelves across the window frame (making sure they're removable for cleaning), then fill them with trailing plants in pots or baskets. You'll undoubtedly sacrifice a certain amount of light, but the sight of the morning sun filtering through the leaves should constitute a more than fair exchange.

As well as providing a welcome oasis of greenery, well-chosen plants can also

Left Where the timber-clad walls meet the pitched ceiling, this attic bedroom has a delightful stencilled border of leaves and lovebirds, facing each other Pennsylvania–Dutch style. For continuous designs like this, clear acetate stencils are easier to work with than those made from metal, plastic, or card.

Above A simple bunch of flowers is the quickest way to add a touch of the country to any room. Here, the real blooms are only part of a *leitmotif* established by the wallpaper, the quilt, and the tapestry cushion. To guard against floral overkill, large areas of plain colour have been provided in the form of white pillowcases and a painted dado area.

add an enchantingly subtle scent of the country to your home; some species of geranium, for example, will release a burst of fragrance every time you brush their leaves. In season, fill bowls, jugs, and vases with fresh flowers. Then, when winter comes, place huge basins of lavender or newly made pot pourri in every room. Instead of harsh chemical sprays, treat your furniture to a coat of beeswax polish, whose delightful essence will linger in the air long after your work is done. However alluring the packaging, don't be tempted by aerosol air fresheners, which, again, are usually full of chemicals, and tend to smell horrid, as well.

Service areas   On a more prosaic note, the most determinedly bucolic home will still need to be heated, so try to choose hardware that has a sympathy with your country mood. If you're undertaking a complete renovation, the ideal choice is an underfloor heating system, which is incredibly efficient as well as being invisible. Where an existing fireplace is the only source of heat, fit a workmanlike solid-fuel stove, many of which will also provide hot water. When radiators cannot be avoided, see if you can find chunky traditional ones – either new or used – which intrude much less on a country scheme than the ugly, modern variety.

If you're stuck with these, you may be able to disguise them behind some kind of open screen, perhaps with a lattice-work construction. At the very least, avoid the common mistake of painting your radiators white; to make them as unobtrusive as possible, colour them to match the wall if it's painted, or, if it's papered, to blend with the pattern as closely as possible.

No matter how much time and care you've taken with your rooms, much of the effort will be wasted if the lighting is poor. Harsh fluorescent strips will kill the effect you're trying to create, so either remove them altogether, or replace them with something more suitable; in a kitchen or bathroom, this may be simple spot fittings, angled to throw light where it's most needed. Almost as deadening as fluorescent fittings are overhead lights of any kind. Again, take them out or replace them; over a dining table, a low-hanging pendant will provide illumination without getting in the way. Elsewhere, choose simple table lamps that cast pools of clear light beside sofas, chairs, and beds, and near storage areas. Supplement these with real oil or hurricane lamps which, although not practical for everyday use, will add a touch of rural atmosphere, and provide a soft, flattering glow when they're lit for special occasions.

Below Few rooms fail to respond to the subtle allure of candlelight; single tapers on their own will make no impact, so gather lots of slender ones together, or display larger specimens in groups of two or three.

Right The reassuringly solid form of old-fashioned radiators is much nicer than the mean, tinny look of modern ones. When a new coat of paint is needed, make sure the metal is completely cold before you begin work, and let the paint dry thoroughly before your radiator is turned on again; if you heat it up too soon, the new surface will blister.

Below In place of curtains, hang a cosy quilt that not only dresses the window, but provides insulation as well. Here, several rows of linked rings form a delicate filigree heading and add length, while some strong picture chain makes an *ad hoc* tie-back.

Below right For a special-occasion lunch, dress your table with a large flowery quilt that will also act as a padded underlay. To protect it, layer white lacy cloths on top, alternating their directions to form a dainty border.

Far right Past the first flush of youth, this padded cane chair was still sturdy and comfortable. As an instant loose cover, we've tossed over a small single-bed quilt that gives it a bright new look and is easy to remove for cleaning.

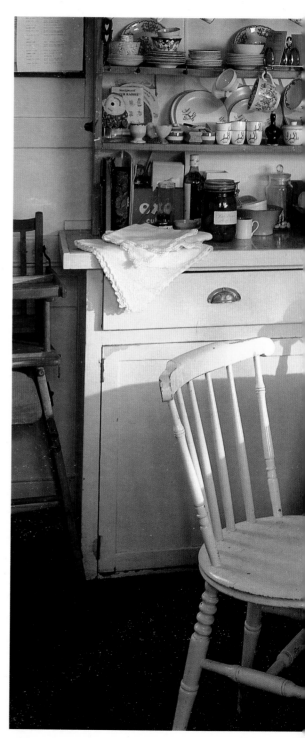

The Fabric of the Country

Everyday objects used in unusual and imaginative ways can add considerable charm to all your rooms, and solve a wide range of design problems at the same time.

To give a subtly rural feeling to your home, find new ways to use and display furnishings or accessories associated with the country look. Baskets, cane tables, small rugs, or jugs of varying sizes are all pretty and versatile, but we've chosen traditional quilts to illustrate a wide range of decorative and practical possibilities.

Old quilts vary widely in price from huge, almost-unused ones, which are very expensive, to the limp, faded cot quilts you can still pick up cheaply in markets and second-hand shops. Whatever you've paid, however, your first priority is to make sure the quilt is clean. To work out how this is best done, first establish the material it's filled with; ordinarily, this is either feathers, old textiles (often blankets), or cottton flock. Surprisingly, those filled with feathers or textiles can, and should, be machine washed (on a cold programme), since handling a heavy, wet quilt can stretch it out of shape; for the same reason, dry it in a tumble dryer on the coolest setting. Unfortunately, flock goes lumpy and matted if it gets wet, so quilts filled in this way should be dry cleaned.

Left Made from delightful old chintz, this gently faded cot cover is filled with feathers and machine quilted in simple squares. To hang it up tapestry fashion, stitch small loops of ribbon, cord, or lace to the back of the top edge, then run a slim rail made from brass piping or gardeners' cane through these loops. Finally, slip the rail into wall-fixed cup hooks.

Below Two colour-coordinated quilts dress this double bed perfectly, yet fulfil very different functions. The coverlet – large and exquisitely hand made – is laid simply over crisp white sheets; the 'headboard' is another machine-made cot quilt tucked and gathered around a top-fixed brass curtain rail – there is no sewing involved. A shelf fixed in this position makes it difficult for the occupants to sit up in bed, but provides a useful surface for night-time paraphernalia when space is tight.

Below A decorative quilt can transform any object of the right height into a coffee or occasional table: a battered trunk, for example, a blanket box, a wicker hamper, a tiny chest of drawers, or even a cardboard carton if it's exceptionally strong. A cot or diminutive single quilt is ideal for a small, low surface, while for one that is larger or higher, you would need a full-sized single or even a double to make sure the edges fall to the floor attractively.

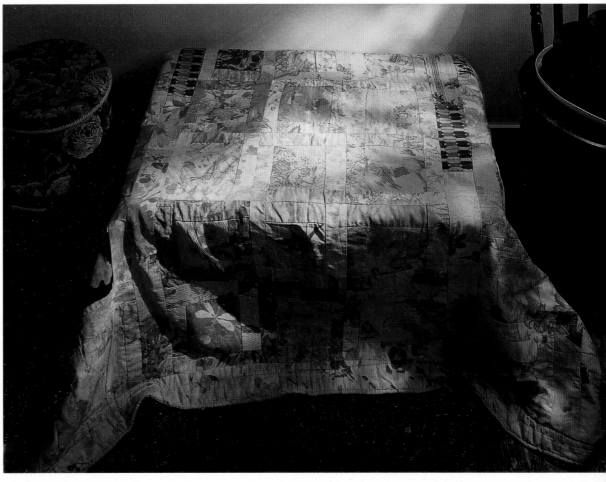

Kitchens and Pantries

Every working kitchen should be equipped for the efficient storage and preparation of food, and for clearing up after meals, and many have to act as a home laundry area as well. Country kitchens, however, seem to take on an additional, almost nurturing role as the emotional heart of the home, and the place where family members naturally gather.

PRACTICAL PLANNING

To fulfil its practical functions, your kitchen must have surfaces that are hardwearing, resistant to moisture, and able to withstand heat. There should be plenty of space to work, adequate storage for supplies and equipment, and a collection of tools, utensils, and accessories that are well designed for their purpose, and appropriate in style for your scheme.

If you don't have a traditional country-kitchen floor made from stone, brick, wood, or ceramic or quarry tiles, choose cork or vinyl in a solid colour or a simple chequerboard pattern. Alternatively, take advantage of the revival in popularity of linoleum, which has all the qualities of vinyl, yet is completely natural in composition. To add a touch of warmth and comfort, lay a washable rug on top (making sure it's backed with purpose-made webbing or underlay so it won't slip and cause an accident), or choose a simple rush mat that can be lifted easily for cleaning.

Typical work surfaces are made from much the same materials: hardwood (like butcher's-block maple), slate, or

Above Plain white-painted timber cladding covers ceiling, walls, and cupboards in a sunny kitchen lit only by skylights.

Left Fresh garden produce, a bowl of eggs, and an old coffee pot full of wooden spoons form a painterly still life in this rustic corner.

ceramic or quarry tiles; if you choose a modern laminate, go for a plain colour. A generous slab of inset marble looks lovely, and makes life easier for the enthusiastic pastry cook.

Nearby walls should have a silk or eggshell finish so they don't absorb grease and are easy to wipe clean. Immediately above the work surface, ceramic tiles are the traditional choice; again, solid colours (especially white) look best, or combine white with a strong primary hue for a bold checked or striped effect – all over, or as a border. Blue-and-white delft-like tiles,

or hand-painted ones with an individual, primitive motif have a suitably rustic feeling, but avoid those designed for assembly into a large sophisticated mural.

The quintessential country appliance is, of course, a huge solid-fuel stove (with a well-worn sofa or easy chair nearby to complete the fantasy). In its absence, a plain white one is best, with refrigerator, washing machine, and other major equipment in a similarly basic form; coloured appliances have an inappropriately fashion-oriented look. A huge, deep, belfast or butler's sink in white glazed stoneware is an ideal choice in terms of style, and extremely useful for washing vegetables and rinsing crockery even if you have a dishwasher; originally, these were supported on a high brick plinth, but they can just as easily be set into a worktop in the usual way. Sinks like this are still being manufactured, but you might prefer to search for an old one; whichever option you choose, brass taps with porcelain handles will complement it perfectly.

FITTINGS & FURNISHINGS

Freestanding furniture rather than fitted units gives a more authentic atmosphere but many people prefer a fitted kitchen, or already have one in place. If this is the case, you can replace existing, perhaps shiny lacquer-finished, doors with simple wooden ones, either new (but without elaborate detailing or shiny varnish) or made up with reclaimed wood from an architectural

salvage yard. Alternatively, fit plain plywood doors yourself, and decorate them with *naif* cut-work designs in the style known as Pennsylvania Dutch. (Dutch in this case is a corruption of *deutsch*, or German.) Typical of this idiom are pairs of birds, flowers, fruit, or animals, facing each other, mirror fashion. The simplest solution of all for cupboard doors is to get rid of an aggressively shiny finish by sanding it down well, then covering it with two coats of oil-based silk or eggshell paint in a solid, or a soft broken, colour, perhaps adding a painted decoration freehand or with a suitable stencil.

If you're planning your kitchen from scratch, consider eschewing fitted units altogether in favour of freestanding furniture. You'll still need a worktop, of course, but open shelves above it would be perfect for showing off gleaming copper or brass pots, pretty china, or foodstuffs in colourful boxes, cans, and packs. Whatever their purpose, kitchen shelves should be made of stout timber, left natural or painted to match the walls; make sure those that hold often-used items are fairly shallow so their contents are easy to see and to reach. For protection, line shelves with pretty paper that you can replace regularly (large lacy doileys maybe), or with PVC-covered cotton, which resembles old-fashioned oilcloth and is easy to wipe clean. If you've

Above If you choose wallpaper for your kitchen, look for a design that is resistant to moisture, or apply a proprietary sealant after the paper is hung. Here, over a traditional butler's sink, a pair of wooden plate racks accommodate dishes of every size.

Right The plain walls of this sunny room have been embellished with a tiny fleur-de-lys motif stencilled in soft grey-blue to match the woodwork and the painted dresser; both of these have a soft eggshell finish whose appealing sheen belies its practicality. Inside the deep window recess, pots of clipped myrtle link the cook's domain with the lush foliage outside.

chosen a decorative lining, extend it over the front to make a border, or fix an attractive edging of ribbon or cotton lace with an adhesive that will peel away easily. In the same position above the work surface, a wall-fixed plate rack is useful for storing, as well as drying, dishes, while an old, wall-hung cupboard with solid or glass doors (a redundant shop fitting, perhaps) will keep dust at bay. For unlovely equipment and cleaning supplies, compromise by fitting closed cupboards underneath your worktop only – or conceal low-level shelves with a curtain made of lightweight, washable fabric that has been gathered onto a slim pole or a length of plastic-coated wire; this wire should be cut slightly shorter than the required length so it stretches to form a straight, taut support.

The most common item of freestanding kitchen furniture is a vast, well-scrubbed table that does double duty for food preparation and, with the addition of a softly faded cotton cloth, for meals. Many of these have a roomy drawer at one end for cutlery or utensils. Another obvious choice is a beautiful old dresser, although originally many of these would have been built in and painted to match the walls; if your kitchen is small, follow tradition and give your dresser the same decorative finish as the rest of the room to make it look less bulky.

Left Everyday crockery, glasses, and trays are stored on a small serving table with a strong shelf above it; always to hand where they're most needed, these items are never out of use long enough to collect dust. Nearby, a deep wall-hung cupboard is ideal for delicate pieces, and those that are rarely required.

Above Freestanding storage furniture has a more authentic country look than modern fitted units; paint it to blend with the walls or to match contrasting mouldings. If you're fitting internal shelves, make sure they're not so far apart that you have to stack china precariously high to avoid wasting space.

To replace standard cupboards, install one or two useful pieces of storage furniture not intended for kitchen use; a sturdy chest of drawers, for example, will accommodate everything from pots and pans to linen and cutlery. Similarly, a capacious wardrobe fitted out with shelves and hooks can hold as much as a small larder, and its resemblance to an *armoire* will provide a touch of Gallic charm. Here again, these items should be stripped and waxed, or given a coat of eggshell paint.

Take care of smaller items by fixing a Shaker-style peg rail across one or more walls; on this you can hang everything from tea towels and aprons to brushes and brooms, from large cooking vessels to string bags full of vegetables. To free the valuable wall space behind a conventional door, replace the door with an idea borrowed from the Old West; saloon-type swing panels (louvres are ideal) that hide the worst of kitchen clutter, yet prevent the cook from feeling cut off, and are easy to push open when your hands are full.

If your kitchen doubles as a laundry,

Above Strongly associated with country kitchens, natural clay quarry tiles are easy to clean, extremely hardwearing, and able to withstand the considerable heat given off by a traditional solid-fuel stove. On the minus side, they can create a great deal of noise in a busy household, and they're cold underfoot unless you have underfloor central heating. In addition, no breakable item dropped on a quarry tile has any chance of survival.

Right Comparatively soft and warm to walk on, vinyl and linoleum also tend to be less expensive than brick, stone, or quarry tiles. Laid in a classic black-and-white chequerboard pattern, they set off polished wood beautifully, and blend in with most country decorating styles. In this cat-infested kitchen, the pastoral look is reinforced with fresh produce displayed in huge stoneware basins.

sort and carry your clothes in big wicker baskets rather than ugly plastic ones – choose those with handles so they can be hung out of the way between wash days. If you don't have an outside clothes line or a tumble dryer, install an old-fashioned overhead clothes airer consisting of several long lengths of dowelling slotted into cast iron ends; this contraption is rigged up on a pulley system so you can lower it to hang wet items, then raise it up while they dry. As well as clothes, an airer like this is ideal for drying flowers and herbs.

WORKING DETAILS

Once the basic elements are in place, reinforce your chosen look by selecting the right equipment and accessories – in addition to fulfilling a practical function, honest well-made items will add greatly to the room's visual appeal.

Country cookware is large and plain; small plain things will do, but avoid any articles decorated with pseudo-country motifs like sheaves of wheat. Pots and pans should be made from copper, enamelled steel, or cast iron, while

Above In its natural timber frame, this supremely practical stable door leads down into the kitchen of a seventeenth-century workman's cottage deep in the English countryside. A neat corner cupboard and wall-hung shelves with curly carved edges supplement the tile-topped storage unit, while a Dutch painted table is laid out with ingredients for making old-fashioned ice cream flavoured with lemons, figs, and scented geranium leaves.

Left Take advantage of otherwise dead space by storing bulky, seldom-used serving pieces on top of cupboards and over doors; similarly, screw a row of brass hooks underneath every possible shelf to hold keys and small utensils as well as cups, mugs, and jugs. Here, the square cupboard on the end wall was originally a meat safe.

Left Conceal low-level storage with fabric instead of cupboard doors; these cheerful checked curtains are made from PVC-covered cotton that is easy to wipe clean and much less expensive than the solid alternative. The 'tiled' splashback is actually wallpaper treated with glossy varnish to resemble a fired glaze.

Below left The kitchen walls, ceiling, and cupboards in this sixteenth-century stone house have been given a soft, parchment-like finish that is the result of careful ragging and sponging; the dark tones of the beams, the furniture, and the woodwork provide contrast.

white or cream earthenware and plain porcelain are best for mixing bowls and baking dishes respectively. For storing dry goods, choose classic pot-bellied glass preserving jars, or those made from pearly salt-glazed French stoneware. Look in flea markets or junk shops for items like painted tin canisters, wooden bins, or classic blue-and-white striped earthenware sets for storing flour, sugar, rice, etc. At one time, chain stores sold huge numbers of these stripey jars, along with larger storage items like bread crocks, and matching tableware, mixing bowls, beakers, and condiment sets.

Collect and display jelly or butter moulds, graceful, friendly jugs, or beautiful old pressed-glass bottles, jars, bowls, and plates. Keep your knives safe and sharp in a wooden box or a wall-hung rack, store your bread in a wooden or stoneware bin, and weigh your cake ingredients in a set of old

Right Rather than being stripped, waxed, and polished, most country furniture would once have had a painted finish. To achieve the kind of rough and rustic look shown here, brush on a layer of paint, then rub most of it off before it dries, or apply a wood stain unevenly.

brass or enamel scales. Keep your eyes open for odd bits of plain or simply patterned crockery; if it's discoloured, you can clean by soaking it overnight in a solution of bleach, denture cleaner, dishwasher powder, or biological detergent. On the wall or ceiling, fix a large rack from which you can hang pots and pans, utensils, ropes of onions or garlic, bunches of herbs, and even home-cured hams.

Often the most attractive displays in a country kitchen are completely natural; leafy herbs clustered on a deep window sill (if you have room, rescue an old water trough or a ceramic sink to hold an indoor herb garden), serried rows of richly coloured preserves, woven baskets or trugs overflowing with fresh fruit and vegetables, and earthenware bowls or wire baskets piled high with finely speckled brown eggs.

Dining Rooms

Whether meals are taken in a large kitchen, at one end of the living area, or in a separate dining room, the ritual of sharing food with family and friends is an important part of country living.

PRACTICAL PLANNING

Clearly, the space you set aside for eating has to contain a surface large enough to accommodate the usual number of diners plus occasional guests, with sufficient room left around it for people to pass, and to pull out their chairs easily.

The floor should be able to withstand the odd splash and spill, so if it's not washable, look for a large rug that can at least be taken up and dry cleaned in case of accidents. A square of rush matting will offer protection against dropped crumbs, but red wine would, of course, go straight through it.

Try to provide a surface nearby from which to serve and clear food (informal country suppers often involve guests helping themselves buffet style), and some form of storage for china, glass, cutlery, and linen.

FITTINGS & FURNISHINGS

A formal, country-house dining room could take a polished walnut or mahogany table, but for most other styles, pine or oak with a simple waxed finish would be more appropriate. Rectangular tables are the usual choice, and they fit most rooms, but if your dining area is suitable, consider a round table instead; those with a centre pedestal can cater for larger numbers,

Above When you're short of space, a small cupboard provides an extra surface for serving, plus storage underneath.

Left A fringed tartan bedspread makes a striking tablecloth that suits the baronial splendour of this candle-lit dining hall.

since they have no legs to fight with those of the diners.

Go for simple wooden chairs, perhaps with ladderbacks or rush seats, or in classic cane or bentwood designs. There's no need for all your dining chairs to match; as long as they're similar in style and material, a collection of odd ones can look charmingly serendipitous. To encourage your guests to linger over coffee, fix tie-on seat pads covered with a homely material like cotton ticking or crisp natural linen. If regular diners are spry enough to clamber in and out easily, replace some or all of your chairs with an old bench, or a church pew.

A sideboard or dresser in a similar wood to the table will provide the necessary serving area and storage space, but a narrow table, desk, or washstand could do the same job; for extra capacity, fix a wall-hung cupboard, corner cupboard, or plate rack above it, or put up a row of shelves with hooks underneath for cups and mugs. If you have a tiny kitchen, but a separate dining room, it makes more sense to keep tableware here, perhaps adapting some of the storage ideas given in the kitchen chapter: a small chest of drawers for linen and cutlery, for example, or a single wardrobe with added shelves for crockery and glasses. A deep shelf at picture (plate) rail height would be ideal to store and display seldom-used serving items like soup tureens and huge platters. If you choose a painted finish for any of your dining room furniture, add a stencilled

Above This welcoming room is subtly lit by single spots fixed to a rough beam.

Above This cheerful breakfast area is strongly French in feeling, with its tiled floor, rough-plastered walls, dark, heavily carved settle, and white porcelain tableware. Crisp cotton tablelinen and simple bunches of wild flowers add freshness and colour.

motif in the form of a pineapple, the early American symbol of hospitality.

WORKING DETAILS

Choose plain white or cream china, supplementing it with odd pieces from junk shops or flea markets; spongeware and spatterware have a nice rustic feel, as do fresh flowery and blue-and-white patterns. A huge basin without its ewer would hold enough salad to feed the largest gathering.

Look out, too, for old cotton tablecloths, perhaps made from material woven in wide checks or stripes, or adorned with charming cross-stitch embroidery. Napkins don't have to match, but they should be similar in feeling, and generous in size.

Avoid formal flower arrangements, and elaborate centrepieces. Bright geraniums in a terracotta pot, a bunch of spring blooms in a jug, or a bowl of shiny fruit would look much nicer.

To bathe your table, and your guests, in a gentle flickering light that is more than adequate for eating, banish electric fittings in favour of candles. If possible, fix a low-hanging chandelier made from brass, tin, iron, or bentwood, or arrange a cluster of candlesticks in the centre of the table. Again, they don't have to match, but they should all be unpretentious in design and made from brass, tin, unadorned earthenware, or turned wood, rather than cut glass or silver; candles, too, should be white or cream, and unscented.

Right An ordinary kitchen table provides a useful surface from which to serve food and drinks. To add light and drama to special meals, supplement the candle on the table with several more scattered around the room.

Right Strongly colonial in style, this family dining room has a cosy feeling that comes from the patina of old wood, the warmth of the large rag rug, and the soft yellow of the architectural detailing. Here, too, a candle sits on the table, while several more hang over it in a chandelier, and reflect off the mirrored back of a wall sconce.

Living Rooms

Of all the rooms in the house, the living room has to cater for the widest range of functions and the largest number of people, so everything in it should be not only attractive to look at, but also simple to use, hardwearing, and easy to clean.

PRACTICAL PLANNING
The basic elements essential in all living rooms are seating, both upholstered and occasional; surfaces, in the form of tables, desks, etc.; and storage, for books, magazines, papers, and video and sound equipment with their accompanying accessories.   If at all possible, arrange the room so it can accommodate more than one activity at a time; some people may want to watch television, for instance, while others would rather chat or play games. These separate areas can be defined, not only by arranging your furniture in companionable L- or U-shaped groupings, but also with rugs. When the room's basic floor covering is a hard surface, or something like coir or sisal that is fairly flat, any kind of rug will do, from a precious oriental carpet to a humble hooked or rag rug, depending on your chosen scheme. If you've fitted pile carpet, however, stick to woven rugs like kelims, dhurries, or druggets, since one pile surface looks odd on top of another.

However it's arranged, make sure there is plenty of seating, with suitable tables nearby so guests don't have to balance plates and cups on their knees. If the dining area is elsewhere, a fairly large table of a similar height would be useful for doing puzzles, playing cards and board games, and, where there's no desk, for writing letters. To avoid a look that has crossed the boundary between casual and untidy, weigh up your storage needs carefully, and provide considerably more capacity than you think you'll need.

Above Upgraded from its original purpose and given a deeply waxed finish, this humble dough bin makes a practical and good-looking occasional table; underneath the hinged lid is a capacious storage area.

Left Combining the best of two worlds, a sleek state-of-the-art computer sits happily on an old kitchen table, surrounded by desk accessories that are sympathetic to the country look: wicker filing baskets, fabric-covered boxes, an old earthenware pen-pot, and a roomy wooden stationery rack. The user-friendly Windsor chair provides plenty of support.

FITTINGS & FURNISHINGS
The upholstered seating in a country house should have proportions that are generous enough to suit both the room and its intended occupants. Above all, it must be comfortable rather than stiff and unyielding; ideally, seat and back cushions should be made from feathers, but best-quality fibre-wrapped foam offers a similar degree of softness. Go for simple, solid shapes rather than curvy, formal ones; traditionally, country chairs and sofas had high backs to keep out draughts, but those who live in modern, centrally heated homes can make decisions about such design details on aesthetic grounds alone. Loose covers are a better choice than tightly fitted ones, since they not only have the right informal look, they are also easy to remove for cleaning.

Although most manufacturers recommend that loose covers be dry cleaned, those made of fabrics like cotton and linen (or linen union, which is a mix of the two) can often be washed successfully on a gentle, cold-water programme. The secret is to replace the covers while they are still damp, so you can stretch them carefully into place. They will then shrink slightly as they dry, smoothing out wrinkles and ensuring a good fit around corners. If your covers have a valance, pleat, or frill around the bottom, this will have to be ironed, and you can either do this *in situ*, or wait until the cover has dried in position, then remove it again to iron the trimming.

If your budget allows, you could even

have two sets of loose covers and change them with the seasons; bleached linen ones for summer perhaps, and a set in dark cosy wool for the colder months. If this is impractical, impart a seasonal look to year-round covers by draping them with a cosy knitted throw in winter and a pale cotton quilt when the weather warms up. Give an upholstered piece with sound springing, but worn or ugly covers, an instant, no-sew transformation by draping it with a large quilt, a blanket, a suitably plain bedspread, or even a hemmed length of fabric; the resulting soft, informal effect is ideal for most country styles.

As well as major items of upholstery, it's a good idea to supply a few occasional chairs. The most typically rustic example of this kind of seating is probably a rocking chair, which seems to give a relaxed atmosphere to any room even when it's not in use. A padded stool or ottoman is another good choice, since it can be moved around as it's needed, and double up as a surface for drinks or newpapers. Where the main eating area is nearby, look for dining chairs that are comfortable enough to be pressed into service when extra guests arrive; cane or bentwood designs with arms and padded seats would be suitably adaptable.

If your living room has a deep bay or bow window, consider building in a roomy window seat. A thick pad and a few throw cushions on top would make this a snug corner for reading, while a hinged lid or doors on the front could transform the inside into a useful cupboard.

Coffee tables are not an authentic country (or period) item, but their usefulness is hard to deny, so aim for an acceptable compromise by finding a low chest or blanket box that will do the same job (and furnish extra storage space at the same time), or look for a

Above The main design feature of this supremely cosy living room is the owner's collection of well-loved antique textiles; at the window, on the floor, and covering both the furniture and an inviting assortment of cushions. To display these textiles to best advantage, the walls have been given an unobtrusive broken-colour treatment in warm green, the furniture has been chosen for its lack of ornamentation, and the accessories have been kept simple, like the brass curtain rail, the unassuming picture frames, and the wicker plant holder and log basket.

small, old (but not valuable) hall or dining table of suitable proportions and cut it down to size.

Higher side tables can be square, rectangular, or round; graceful Shaker candle stands on their delicate pedestals are an ideal choice in small rooms. Disguise a table that has seen better days under a cotton, chenille or quilted cloth, or even a woollen throw or silk shawl. The trick is to make the covering look casual and uncontrived, so at all costs avoid embellishing any table with one of the full-length fitted and frilled chintz frocks so beloved of decorators.

In many living rooms, built-in shelving provides most of the storage space; make sure yours is strong and thick, both to take the considerable weight of books and records, and to avoid the mean, temporary, look of thin planks. If necessary, fix a deep edging to increase their apparent weight, and unless your shelves are built from particularly beautiful timber, paint them to match the walls, allowing their contents to provide visual interest.

WORKING DETAILS

To give your living room an instant touch of softness and comfort, provide several inviting piles of assorted — not matching or coordinating — cushions. You can make many of these yourself using old curtains or the sound portions of worn quilts, rugs, or carpets. To cope with materials as thick as these, you'll need stout shears, strong twine, and either a heavyweight needle on your sewing machine, or an upholsterer's half-circle needle if you want to do the job by hand. When you've finished stitching, trim the seams well back, and cut across the corners so they'll lie flat.

Even if there is no fireplace in your living room, install a huge wicker log basket into which you can throw

Above The dazzling yellow-and-green scheme in this modest cottage was inspired by the saucer-sized sunflowers that grow nearby. To provide visual relief from a potentially overpowering expanse of pure colour, the internal door has been stripped and waxed, and the floor has been covered with medieval-style matting made from plaited rush. Note the characteristic tripod table, a common feature in old country cottages because of its stability.

Left Wallpaper printed with palest apricot stripes makes the perfect backdrop to an informal display of antique plates with a posy of old roses in an heirloom beaker. Plain white candles cast a soft light without competing for attention.

Above More than a hint of Swedish influence is evident in this country-house drawing room with its imposing proportions; while the metal-framed sofas, the attenuated candlesticks, and the arrangement of empty picture frames are unmistakably contemporary, the pale limed floor, the filmy white curtains, and the fresh blue-and-white stripes are pure Carl Larsson.

newspapers and magazines, or toys. Smaller baskets too are much more appropriate (and cheaper) for holding plants than elaborate *jardinières* or *cache-pots*, and, in a cottage-style room, you could even hang large, flat baskets or trays on the wall instead of pictures.

Unless you have a manor-house drawing room that cries out for family portraits, hunting prints, and botanical drawings, other suitable wall decorations are hand-stitched samplers,

primitive portraits, or tapestries
worked in needlepoint or embroidery.

In terms of lighting, simple modern
table fittings in wood, earthenware, or
brass are better than fancy reproduction
designs or those transformed into lamps
from other objects like bottles and jars.
To make sure the light is not distorted,
choose white or cream shades; brand-
new ones can be given a streaky aged
look if you brush them lightly with
thinned matching emulsion paint.

Above A subtle blue-green stain brings out the
lovely grain of the timber panelling that
dominates this elegant colonial room. Fixed
over the fireplace are a pair of unusual candle
sconces protected by glass shades, but everyday
illumination comes from a brass table lamp with
a plain cream shade that won't distort the light.

Bedrooms

Country bedrooms come in a wide range of styles, from the flowery exuberance of the English country-house look to the almost monastic simplicity of a Provençal chamber with its bare floorboards and wall-hung cross. Because this room is a private retreat for sleeping, grooming, and relaxing at the end of the day, its scheme is not limited by all the practical considerations necessary in other, more public, rooms.

PRACTICAL PLANNING

Even the most basic bedroom in constant use should contain a bed and enough storage space to accommodate clothing, accessories, and grooming equipment. Of these elements, the largest is likely to be the bed, so it's best to establish where this will go first, then arrange the other furnishings around it. In Britain and the United States, beds are usually positioned with the head against a wall, jutting out into the room; in France, however, they are often placed against a wall side-on. This arrangement certainly makes better use of space, but before you decide on it, make sure no noise comes through from the adjoining room, and fit the bed with castors so you can roll it out when you need to make it, or clean the floor underneath.

You'll want something soft and warm under your bare feet, so if the room has floor boards, or a scratchy covering like sisal or rush, find a small rug to go beside the bed.

As with kitchens, freestanding

Above Generously gathered curtains of filmy muslin give a light, romantic, and country-fresh look to a huge four-poster bed; note the dainty self-pelmet that reinforces the frame's graceful dome.

Left Clad in similar but less elaborate drapery, this white bed is typical of colonial style. Other signature features in this Mount Vernon room are the wide-plank floor, the contrasting woodwork, and the simple portraits.

storage is more authentic than fitted units, although if space (and/or money) is tight, you could get away with fixing shelves and hanging rails across one entire wall, then covering them with floor-to-ceiling, wall-to-wall curtains in unbleached cotton or a similarly plain, cheap fabric.

(Guest bedrooms can make do with very little storage space; one small chest would be enough, with hanging capacity furnished by a sturdy hat stand,

or a row of brass hooks and hangers.)

Where there's room, an easy chair with a reading light nearby provides a quiet corner away from the hurly burly of family life.

Many traditional country bedrooms have their own small fireplaces; if yours has been blocked up, fill the grate with sweet-smelling cones or bunches of dried flowers. If it's still in working order, though, treat yourself occasionally to a real fire, making sure the guard is in position so that you can drift off to sleep in the rosy glow of dying embers.

FITTINGS & FURNISHINGS

Manor-house beds may be hung with yards of chintz or lace, but for most other country styles, a modest design in brass, wrought iron or turned wood is more in keeping; you might even find an old utility or institutional bed at a knock-down price. If you are attracted to an old bedstead, measure it to make sure you can buy a new mattress that fits. (Never buy an old mattress, since it will have taken on the shape of its previous owner.)

For a French country look, choose a wooden bed with high, curved head- and footboards; in English this is known as a sleigh bed, but the French call it a *bateau lit*.

If you have a simple divan, either find a homely wooden headboard for it, or hang a small quilt or rug behind it to give a similar effect. Avoid fancy quilted or padded designs, though, especially those that match the curtains

Left Although this scheme is strongly modern in feeling, it is also anchored in the colonial style, with its hinged wall lights and tailored valances. The predominance of pure white and the nautical-stripe sheets and pillowcases give this cool bedroom a distinct flavour of the seaside.

Left A delightful mix of geometric motifs in pretty blue-and-white – striped blinds and wallpaper, checked coverlet and valance, and a folded quilt stitched and appliquéd with triangles – dominates this sunny corner; to complement these the bedside table has been given a neat fitted cloth made from classic grid-pattern tea towels, and smartly piped along the seams.

Above In addition to the gingham fabrics in this large country-house bedroom, the limed floorboards, the timber-framed period furniture, and the stripey rug all suggest a scheme inspired by Carl Larsson's Scandinavian style. Here, built-in cupboards with traditional detailing make efficient use of the fireplace alcoves.

or bed cover, since this designer idiom is too contrived to have a real country feel — you're better off doing without altogether.

To add a subtle, fragrant touch, tie a spray of lavender or herbs to your bedhead with a bit of ribbon or lace.

Beside the bed, you'll need a table. Look for an old one made from cane or wood, or use a small wicker or tin trunk instead, which offers additional space inside for storage.

Wardrobes and chests are likely to be made from pine or oak, left natural, or painted; again, only grand country-house rooms would suit polished timbers. Sale rooms are often filled

with blackish, heavy-looking oak furniture that, if its basic shape is good, can be transformed by stripping it of its dingy varnish.

If hanging space is tight, store out-of-season clothing in large wicker hampers stacked in a corner, or on top of the wardrobe, or use one of these for dirty laundry.

If grooming is to be carried on here, you'll need a surface for jars and bottles, a large mirror and somewhere to sit. A sturdy table or desk with a wooden chair is a much better choice than a kidney-shaped dressing table decked out with frilly skirts and matching stool. To relieve pressure on

work. (Or add a delicate border yourself by stitching narrow cotton lace along the edges of sheets and pillowslips.) As well as looking authentic, white is a very practical choice since it won't clash with any other design element. What's more, because all the pieces match, you are never left with odd items when some wear out. If you really want a pattern, choose fresh checks or stripes, but steer clear of large flowery or other, more exotic, motifs. When you're folding freshly washed bedlinen, tuck in one or two scented sachets to add a subtle hint of lavender or rose or other flower-fresh smell.

As well as being warm and easy to use, duvets have the same comfortable plumpness as traditional eiderdowns. Pure woollen blankets also look nice, especially when they're finished off with a crisp top sheet neatly folded over.

Coverlets should not be silky or frilled; a large quilt would be ideal, of course, but a plain throwover cover of white or cream crochet, cotton, linen, or even candlewick, is fine, as well. If you want a valance on your bed, it should be plain, and straight or gently gathered. To make a charming valance from cotton lace, look out for one of the narrow widths with finished hems, and gather a length of this around the edge of a square of curtain lining slightly narrower than your bed. Then place the lining between the mattress and its divan base so the lace hangs down to the floor.

For an appealing collection of bedroom cushions, make covers from lace place-mats, tray cloths, antimacassars, or large handkerchiefs. To produce a dainty, charming cushion cover almost instantly, slip an appropriately sized feather pad inside a folded nightdress or pyjama case, then stitch the opening by hand.

Above A dark attic corner has been made cosy and cheerful by the use of prettily sprigged paper on the walls and ceiling, blossom-strewn fabric at the window, and sympathetically flowery accessories scattered around. Pushed against the wall in the French manner, the curvy single bed is made up with pristine white bedlinen.

the bathroom, a small bedroom basin is invaluable; choose a white one, and conceal it behind a pretty screen made from fabric gathered onto a wooden frame, or set it into an old washstand that would originally have held an earthenware ewer and basin for morning ablutions.

WORKING DETAILS
Purists would insist that bedlinen is made from white cotton or linen, perhaps adorned with drawn thread-

Left Floral motifs are one of the most popular of all country decorating themes. Here, as well as adorning china, fabrics, cushions, and rugs, flowers appear as the common subject of a charming collection of pictures that encircle the room. The lacy canopy on the four-poster is a large bedcover trimmed with Chinese cut-work lace.

Right This tiny chamber has plain pale walls and a coir-covered floor that enlarge it visually and focus attention on the enchanting wrought-iron and brass bed and dramatic full-length curtains.

Children's Rooms

While adult bedrooms have comparatively few demands made on them, children's rooms have to be flexible and tough as well as attractive, since they usually double up as play areas.

PRACTICAL PLANNING

Children often have very strong ideas about their environment, so if you make an effort to involve them at the planning stage, they'll be happier to sleep, play, and entertain their friends, in the finished room.

On the floor, the ideal surface should be washable and resilient, but not so hard that it will cause injury to stumbling tots and dropped toys; washable carpet, perhaps cord or carpet squares, for example, vinyl or linoleum, or cork would be fine. For slightly older children, lay down sheets of hardboard that can be painted to resemble a farmyard, a giant railway, a draughts (checkers) board or whatever else might interest them.

Below There are very few items of furniture that need to be provided in scaled-down form, but among these are a baby's cot, and one or two toddler-sized chairs. Here, a chest of drawers at the small end of the adult-size range is perfect for a child's room permanently occupied by a family of old-fashioned painted and stuffed dolls.

The most practical wall treatment (and suitably rustic in its simplicity) is paint with a washable finish; plain walls also form a neutral background for the inevitable jumble of clothing, pictures, toys, and games.

There are an increasing number of wallpaper designs available for children, but if you choose one of these, you may have to redecorate within a few years since youngsters are capable of inflicting considerable damage. In addition, their tastes change quickly – a room covered in fluffy bunnies may suddenly provoke howls of protest from a tough five-year-old.

If you want some form of decoration on your walls, choose a wallpaper that is not overly babyish, and hang it above dado (chair) rail height only, leaving the most vulnerable, lower part of the wall plain, or protected with timber cladding. Better still, add interest to painted walls with stencils or freehand designs, which can be easily obliterated when it's time for a change.

FITTINGS & FURNISHINGS

There's no need to fit out a child's room with scaled-down furniture which is unnecessarily expensive, quickly outgrown, and a bit twee for the country look. Instead, buy only those small items that are absolutely necessary (a cot or crib in wood or iron, and a toddler-sized chair) and select everything else from an adult range that

Right For an older child, it's important to provide study and relaxation facilities as well as space for well-loved toys and games. In this early-American bedroom in Philadelphia, a painted trunk serves as a surface for display as well as a capacious storage facility, while an unusual antique model is wall-hung so it takes up no room and stays out of harm's way.

Left A colour-wash of candy pink brings cheer to a children's room and makes a sympathetic background for the bright colours of their books, toys, and drawings. Here again, this two-drawer table will serve as a useful desk when crayons are exchanged for pencils and pens.

Left A soft rug on top of coir matting provides a surface that's kind to crawling infants and tumbling tots, while parents will appreciate an upholstered armchair at story time. When it comes to decoration, a wide paper border establishes the zoological theme that dominates the room.

is straightforward in design so each piece can be adapted for different uses as the child grows; a sturdy coffee table, for instance, is the ideal height for a toddler to sit at for drawing, an older child to kneel at for games, and a teenager to use for a kettle and mugs. In the same way, a full-sized wardrobe can be fitted with an extra shelf in the middle to make the best use of space.

In the past, nurseries were furnished largely with bits and pieces no longer needed elsewhere, like a battered sofa that childish imaginations could transform into a besieged fort, a trusty steed, or a tossing galleon, or a scuffed dining table that additional scratches or paint spills couldn't harm. The one item that should never be handed down, though, is a bed; a growing child requires the support of a good, new mattress, but again, there's no need for a special size – as soon as the cot gets too small, replace it with a standard single bed that will last into adulthood, perhaps with a roll-out trundle arrangement underneath for friends.

To avoid untidiness, make sure there's plenty of storage: wicker baskets and wooden chests are nicer in a country room than brightly coloured plastic boxes. Shelves, fitted or freestanding, will provide a home for stuffed toys and games as well as books. At child's shoulder height, fix a Shaker peg rail on which to hang clothing and bags of toys.

WORKING DETAILS

If your floor covering is hard, you'll need area rugs for warmth and comfort. Choose washable ones, or go for colonial-style floor cloths, which are just squares of heavy canvas given coats of primer, paint, and varnish. They're fairly easy to make at home, especially if you keep them small so you can work on the kitchen table. For decoration, use chubby letters spelling out your child's name, or enlarge the image of a favourite cartoon character.

Furry animals, wooden toys, and dolls have a more natural look than plastic models and computer games, so leave these on constant display. Look for an old-fashioned dolls' house, a set of farmyard animals, or, the most traditional of all country toys, a rocking horse; originally, this was not merely a plaything, it was a valuable teaching aid used to familiarize children with the only available means of transport.

Above An enlarged detail of the room opposite reveals a row of whimsical hooks sensibly fixed where children can reach them; at a similar height, a single hook on the back of the door makes use of otherwise wasted space.

Bathrooms

The ideal country-style bathroom is a perfect combination of traditional charm with modern warmth and efficiency. It should be simple without being clinical, yet pretty and comfortable at the same time.

PRACTICAL PLANNING

While kitchen surfaces have to withstand moisture in the form of steam, those in the bathroom are often exposed to direct contact with water as well.

Floors should be made of wood, ceramic tiles, plain vinyl or linoleum, or natural cork. Fitted carpet isn't strictly appropriate, but you can add a softening touch with a small washable rug or a flat cotton bath mat.

Plain walls are best, especially in a small steamy space, but if your heart is set on paper, choose one that is resistant to moisture; in a large room (many country bathrooms are converted from bedrooms), an ordinary paper may do, if you protect it with a proprietary sealant or two coats of matt polyurethane varnish. Around the bath and basin, a surface of classic tiles has the right look, perhaps with a border of odd Victorian specimens.

FITTINGS & FURNISHINGS

The most authentic sanitary fittings for a country bathroom (and the most practical for most other styles as well) are plain white ones in basic shapes.

Traditional vast roll-top baths made from porcelain-coated cast iron are difficult to find, expensive to buy, and

Above In the tiny bathroom of this seventeenth-century cottage, the basin is fitted with traditional brass mixer taps; note their porcelain-trimmed handles whose cross-head design makes them easy to grip with wet hands.

Left A painted finish is the best choice for most bathroom walls. Here, a soft cloud-like effect has been achieved by applying a base of pale sky-blue, then dragging it with off-white using a mixture of glaze and eggshell paint.

much too heavy for most bathrooms that aren't on the ground floor. Modern acrylic models are warm to the touch and very light, but they can be costly as well, and they're not really suited to country rooms; the best choice is also the cheapest, and the most common – enamelled pressed steel. Look for a size that is big enough to be comfortable without taking up unnecessary space and requiring wasteful amounts of

water to fill it. Cover the side panel with the same tiles used on the wall or the floor, or with painted timber cladding.

Basins can be set in (to a purpose-made unit, or an old washstand, table, or sideboard), wall-hung, or, as is most often the case, supported on a pedestal; a gathered skirt attached with velcro will disguise an ugly pedestal and provide a hidden storage area for cleaning materials and toilet rolls. Above the basin, hang a plain or wood-framed mirror tall enough to cater for family members of varying heights.

Look for an old wooden smokers' chest to hold small toiletries, and fix it to the wall using strong mirror plates; for larger items, as well as towels and face cloths, try to fit in a small wooden chest of drawers, or even a cane table with shelves underneath. A wood, cane or Lloyd Loom chair would be handy for discarded clothing.

WORKING DETAILS

To blend in with your country scheme, provide simple accessories made from wood or brass. A freestanding rail for towels is ideal, but if space is limited, hang them on a single long length of dowelling or brass tubing, fixed above the bath or across one whole wall.

Towels should be plain rather than patterned, and, predictably, white. Near the basin, provide one or two small ones made from snowy linen with an edging of lace or drawn threadwork. Ready-made shower curtains are often printed with bright modern patterns, so

Left Polished wooden furniture is suitable only in large bathrooms where moisture from steam and condensation are unlikely to cause damage.

Left Stencilled motifs based on early-American designs are framed by the dark beams in this English cottage bathroom.

sew one yourself in a suitable fabric backed with clear or white plastic.

Keep sponges, loofas, and small bottles and jars in open baskets; pretty, small junk shop plates and bowls (in glass or earthenware) make dainty soap dishes, while cream-sized jugs will hold combs or toothbrushes. A large jug or a basinless ewer makes an elegant container for the lavatory brush.   Drawings and prints may not appreciate exposure to a damp atmosphere, so hang a collection of decorative plates on the wall instead. Similarly, this is not the best environment for cut or dried flowers, but plants will thrive, especially if there's plenty of light. Choose sweet-smelling herbs or fragrant species like jasmine or scented-leaf pelargonium, whose essence will be released in the moist heat.

Below All-white schemes give an impression of purity and cleanliness; when every surface is washable, white is a practical choice. In this cool monochrome setting, a spiky plant and a twig rocker become sculptural objects.

Above Buttery gold walls, heirloom accessories, and rich textiles give this country-house bathroom an atmosphere of warmth and luxury.

Right Make a display of your most interesting soaps and toiletries by storing them in pretty old pieces of china and glass.

Designing the Country Look   89

Halls, Stairs, and Landings

The first (and last) impression visitors have of your home will usually come from the entrance hall, the adjoining stairs, and perhaps the landing beyond, yet their design can easily be overlooked when all your thoughts are being concentrated elsewhere.

These areas act as a link between rooms, so it's a good idea to give them all the same decorative treatment; since they're often narrow and dark, choose a rich, warm colour like ochre yellow, old rose, or even pale terracotta. In old country houses, entrance halls were often built from great stone blocks, so if your home is appropriate in size, age, and location, you might like to duplicate this look with a *trompe l'œil* paint effect; think twice, though, if you live in a modern box or a tiny Victorian town house, where such a grand treatment could look faintly ridiculous.

Above In country manor-houses, the hall is often big enough to act as an extra room. Here, an unusual Malaysian bench is dwarfed by a tree-like arrangement of poplar and trachelium.

Right A perfect mix of elegance and practicality, this welcoming entrance has a stone-flagged floor and a thick door curtain on a hinged rail to keep out wintry draughts. Nearby, a collection of hats, bags, and walking sticks sits ready for use.

Flooring should be tough and easy to clean; if it's not a traditional hard surface like brick, stone, or tiles, make sure there's a large mat or rug in front of outside doors to absorb the first, muddiest, footprints.

Most modern halls are too small to contain much in the way of furniture, but if there's room, an old wooden settle, a simple bench, or just a small chair would be useful when you need to remove wet shoes. To hold bulky outdoor garments, choose a large, curvaceous coat stand, or screw a row of strong brass hooks into a length of wall-fixed timber.

A hall table is handy for dumping keys, gloves, bags, and letters, but if space is a problem, put up a deep wooden shelf instead; *in extremis*, a bicycle pannier suspended from a single hook would be better than nothing.

On the wall, install a large wooden-framed mirror for last-minute grooming checks, and look for an old barometer, which will add a genuine flavour of rural life since keeping track of the weather is of vital importance to most country dwellers.

Near the door, a stand for umbrellas and walking sticks, a row of rubber boots, and a big wicker dog basket, will fulfil a range of useful functions.

Above right The unexpectedly deep pink of this farmhouse hall successfully draws together the grey stone floor, the dark polished furniture, and the larchwood ceiling beams. To achieve this colour, lime was mixed with raddle – the dye used for marking sheep.

Right An arched stone porch with integral seat shelters this massive doorway from inclement weather.

Above A potentially dismal stairwell has been transformed into a tropical grotto with a coat of rose-pink paint and a collection of crimson and scarlet blooms interspersed with exotic fruits. For summer lunches, a brilliantly hued batik and complementary kelim add a touch of softness.

Garden Rooms

Whether it's an authentic Victorian conservatory or a small glazed lean-to, a garden room of some kind provides a retreat from the world that's filled with the light, the colour, and the fragrance of the country.

If you're installing such a structure yourself, make sure it's in keeping with the style of your house; a huge Gothic fantasy, for example, would look absurd stuck on the side of a modern suburban dwelling. Although it involves additional cost, consider putting in full central heating to benefit both the resident plants and the room's human occupants, who could then make use of it all year round. Nowhere is it written that conservatories must be white on the outside; dark green is equally traditional and it blends more sympathetically with massed foliage.

If it's to have a practical, horticultural function, your garden room needs a floor that's completely impervious to water, so it should be made from stone or brick, or ceramic, quarry, or concrete tiles. Efficient drainage is essential. Walls, too, will have to withstand considerable moisture, so painted surfaces are best; choose a pale, unassuming colour that will provide a sympathetic background for flowers and plants.

Furniture should be simple in shape,

Right More an extra living area than a conservatory, this snug garden room is floored with layered kelims and hung with masses of stripey fabric to keep it cool on sunny days. Underneath a hanging Regency bird cage, a sturdy cricket table holds a jug full of garden flowers.

unaffected by damp, and made from natural materials like cane or unpolished wood; although a popular choice for many modern settings, plastic furniture looks wrong in a country-garden room. Cast iron tables and chairs would be a good choice, though, as would their modern equivalents made from steel or aluminium, which are both lighter and less prone to rust. Here again, painted conservatory furniture often looks nicer in green, or a pretty mix of ice-cream pastels, than in stark white.

Taking meals in a garden room is one of its greatest pleasures; if yours isn't big enough to accommodate a table full-time, look for a folding one that can be tucked away when it's not needed.

As with house plants, choose comparatively local, rather than exotic, species and cultivate them in wooden tubs or real terracotta pots; vast, terrace-sized ones make a dramatic impact, and require less frequent watering. Display small specimens on tiered metal stands or built-in shelves, and train an enormous vine to clamber up the walls and across the ceiling.

For decoration, nestle decoy birds among sturdy branches. At night, tuck chunky white candles in flower pots among the plants so their dappled light casts enchanting shadows.

Left Rough-plastered walls, an old quarry-tile floor, and curly chairs made from cane and wrought iron give this English country conservatory a strong Provençal look. Fixed on the wall, a Victorian mantel mirror reflects the maximum amount of light, while underneath it, a marble wash-stand makes an impervious surface for potted plants.

Creating the Country Look

Flying Finish—*A Round-up of Techniques*   96

Freckled Finish—*Spattering a Picture Frame*   102

Lamp Light—*Sponging a Lampbase*   104

The Bronze Age—*Verdigris on a Chair*   106

Art of Deception—*Trompe l'œil on a Trunk*   108

Window Dressing—*Stencilling Around a Window*   110

Old from New—*Antiquing a Pair of Kitchen Chairs*   112

A Polished Performance—*Lacquering a Table*   114

Ways with Wood—*Woodgraining a Door*   116

Floor Effects   118

A Fiery Focus—*Tiling Around a Fireplace*   122

Chequered Footnote—*Laying an Inlay Floor*   124

First Impressions—*A Floor Painted
                            after the Style of Matisse*   126

The Material World   128

Decorative Details   132

Quilt Edged—*Making a Patchwork Throw*   136

Colourful Cushions—*Two Appliqué Designs*   138

Creations with Contrast   140

Something from Scraps—*Making a Rug from Rags*   142

Fire Highlighter—*Creating a Firescreen
                            from Scraps of Fabric*   144

Flying Finish

A Round-up of Techniques

Country decorating is about furniture, floors, objects, and walls *inside* the home – and how they reflect and echo 'the great outdoors'. Appropriate colours and a few simple skills, such as painting, if combined with resource-fulness and practicality, can help to create an authentic 'countryside' ambience in any room in the house.

COLOURWASHING

This gives walls a translucent, dappled quality. Pale shades are especially suited to this technique, creating a fresh, airy look which can brighten up the gloomiest of rooms.

Technique You can use either water-based or oil-based paints as the top coat for colourwashing but since water-based emulsion dries faster, it allows a more rapid build-up of colour.

Apply a base coat of eggshell or vinyl silk emulsion and leave it to dry. Thin the 'colourwash' paint to a milky consistency using the appropriate solvent with the chosen colour added. Brush the colourwash loosely and roughly over the surface and, while it is still wet, gently rub using a clean cloth.

When the first layer of colour has dried, repeat the process. Dry over night before applying a second coat.

SPONGING

This is a simple technique which creates a dappled finish on walls and furniture.

Technique You can use a vinyl silk emulsion or eggshell for the base coat.

Dragging

Apply the base coat and allow to dry. Thin and tint the top colour, using oil-based or water-based paint, and dab some of it onto a natural sponge. Press over the surface.

Allow the paint to dry and continue until the whole area is completed.

STENCILLING

A stencil is a patterned motif, usually copied onto plain surfaces. It is an effective way to break up large areas of flat colour on walls, floors, and furniture.

Technique   Design your own stencil onto a stencil card or acetate, or buy a ready-cut kit. The chosen surface should be dry and already painted in the base colour. When cutting out the stencil, try to be as precise as possible.

Pencil in registration marks over the area to be stencilled. Attach the stencil to the beginning of the pattern area with masking tape or adhesive spray.

Dab a little of the first colour onto the surface through the stencil, building up the colour slowly and allowing it to dry before removing the stencil and attaching it to the next spot. Repeat this process until the area to be stencilled in this and any other colours has been completed. Finally, coat with clear varnish.

RAGGING

Ragging creates a soft-textured, broken finish on walls and furniture. It is a simple technique which involves a rag being rolled in different directions to give ripples of colour.

Technique   You can use either water-based or oil-based paints and glazes for ragging.

Apply a base coat and leave it to dry. Thin the paint or glaze for 'ragging' with the appropriate solvent and add

Stippling

some colour. Apply with a wide soft brush, leaving about 5mm ($\frac{1}{4}$in) at the top and sides of the area being ragged. Then use a small dry brush to stipple the paint into the edges. Soak a rag in the paint and wring it out, then dab onto the surface in a figure-of-eight movement. Continue until the area to be ragged is completed, keeping the rag at the same wet consistency and wringing it out when necessary.

DRAGGING

Dragging is a series of graduated lines which emerge on a monochrome background as a brush is pulled through wet glaze. As this effect can sometimes give a formal look, be careful how you use it in a country setting.

Technique   You can use oil-based or water-based paints and glazes for dragging, but since oil-based glazes dry out more slowly than water-based emulsions, they are easier to work with.
   Apply a base coat of eggshell or vinyl silk emulsion and leave it to dry. For the 'dragging' colour, thin and tint an oil-based glaze. Now paint a vertical band of colour from the ceiling to the skirting board, keeping the glaze thin. While the paint is still wet, drag a dry wide brush down the wall. The base colour should appear through the brushed stripes. Continue until the area to be dragged is completed.

STIPPLING

Stippling breaks up paint to give an even, lightly speckled effect, achieved by taking a densely bristled 'stippling' brush over newly applied paint.

Technique   You can use eggshell or vinyl silk emulsion for the base coat. Both water-based and oil-based paint or glaze can be used for the 'stippling' but oil-based eggshell is less absorbent than emulsion and easier to work with.

Apply the base coat and leave it to dry. For the top coat, thin and tint an oil-based glaze and apply it to the prepared area. Now press a stippling brush or textured roller against the wet glaze and lift off – the base colour should show and lighten the glaze.

SPATTERING

Spattering is a technique in which flecks of coloured paint are sprayed over a surface to give it a 'speckled' finish which is less dense than stippling. It is simple to do and can be used on any type of surface, smooth or textured.

Technique   You can use oil-based or water-based paints. It is messy, so make sure everything in the immediate area is well protected.

Apply a base coat using eggshell or vinyl silk emulsion and leave it to dry. Thin the paint to a flickable consistency and tint to your chosen colour. Dip a dry brush in the paint mixture and hold it parallel and reasonably close to the surface to be spattered (about 15cm/6in should give an even spatter but distances will vary depending on the size of area you wish to cover). Run your fingers through the bristles towards the surface, to release a spray of tiny dots over the area. Repeat until the surface is evenly covered.

VERDIGRIS

Natural verdigris is caused by the corrosion of copper, brass, and bronze but the authentic green, crumbly saltiness can be imitated by applying this special paint finish to all surfaces.

Technique   Prepare the chosen surface with an oil-based or water-based primer.

Buy or mix up a copper paint, loosely

apply it onto the surface and leave it to
dry. Choose two shades of green and
paint the paler shade onto the surface
first. Don't cover the copper-coloured
paint completely – some should be
allowed to show through.

ANTIQUING

Antiquing re-creates the effect of years
of wear and tear on paint, wood, and
plaster. This aged look can be given to
walls, floors, and furniture with
striking effect.

Technique   Use either water-based
or oil-based paints for antiquing.
   Apply a couple of layers of base coat,
using eggshell or vinyl silk, and leave it
to dry. Thin the chosen paint with the
appropriate solvent and tint to the
desired colour – duller earth colours
are the most effective. Apply to the
surface and leave to dry before applying
a second coat in a similar but not
identical colour. When the second coat
is dry, gently rub back the painted
surface in areas with sandpaper, so that
the base coat shows through.

WOODGRAINING

Woodgraining is a decorative technique
which imitates the flow of natural
woodgrain. The effect can give an
authentic 'woody' look to walls, doors,
floors, and furniture.

Technique   Surfaces must be free
from dirt and grease, so wipe with a
clean rag. Oil-based paints and glazes
are most suitable for this technique
since they are non-porous and dry
slowly, allowing the area to be worked
on for a longer period of time.
   Apply two base coats of eggshell in a
colour that resembles a pale shade of
wood. Thin and tint an oil-based glaze –
use a shade darker than the base coat.

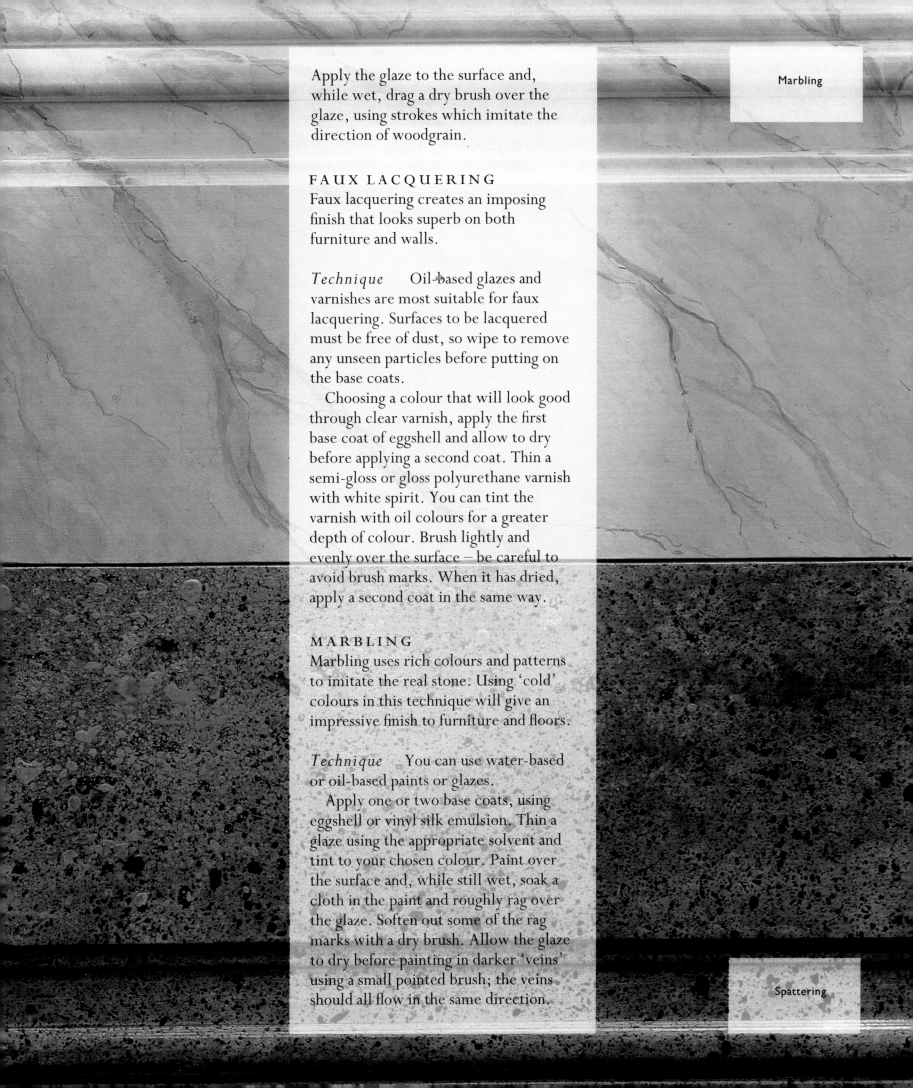

Apply the glaze to the surface and, while wet, drag a dry brush over the glaze, using strokes which imitate the direction of woodgrain.

FAUX LACQUERING

Faux lacquering creates an imposing finish that looks superb on both furniture and walls.

Technique   Oil-based glazes and varnishes are most suitable for faux lacquering. Surfaces to be lacquered must be free of dust, so wipe to remove any unseen particles before putting on the base coats.

Choosing a colour that will look good through clear varnish, apply the first base coat of eggshell and allow to dry before applying a second coat. Thin a semi-gloss or gloss polyurethane varnish with white spirit. You can tint the varnish with oil colours for a greater depth of colour. Brush lightly and evenly over the surface – be careful to avoid brush marks. When it has dried, apply a second coat in the same way.

MARBLING

Marbling uses rich colours and patterns to imitate the real stone. Using 'cold' colours in this technique will give an impressive finish to furniture and floors.

Technique   You can use water-based or oil-based paints or glazes.

Apply one or two base coats, using eggshell or vinyl silk emulsion. Thin a glaze using the appropriate solvent and tint to your chosen colour. Paint over the surface and, while still wet, soak a cloth in the paint and roughly rag over the glaze. Soften out some of the rag marks with a dry brush. Allow the glaze to dry before painting in darker 'veins' using a small pointed brush; the veins should all flow in the same direction.

Spattering

Freckled Finish
Spattering a Picture Frame

Spattering is an ideal way to create interest in a relatively small surface area, and you can vary its effects dramatically according to the number of colours you use.

We have chosen to spatter an old picture frame, but this technique could equally add interest to a more modern frame, for family photographs, perhaps. Choose your colour scheme to fit in with the pictures you want to frame; the choice of paint colours is much wider than the choice of frames in a framing shop, so you can get exactly the right tone.

One The frame must be clean and free from grease or wax, so wipe thoroughly with a clean rag. Give it a coat of acrylic wood primer, then fill in any remaining holes with an all-purpose filler. Allow the filler to dry before finally sanding down the surface. Paint will spatter everywhere, so cover the immediate area with plenty of newspapers or paper towels. Or paint outside if the weather is fine.

Two This frame was given a base coat of ready-mixed yellow vinyl silk emulsion – ideal for a decorative surface that will not receive a lot of hard use. (If you're using this finish on furniture or floors that will take some hard knocks, however, you'll probably find oil-based paints tougher and more durable.)

Three For our spatter effect, we mixed equal quantities of black and burnt umber artists' acrylic paint with water to a single cream consistency. Dab a 2.5cm (1in) brush in the mixed colour, removing any excess paint to avoid blobs building up when it is spattered. Holding the brush in line with the frame, run your fingers through the bristles towards the frame – the paint will spray across and onto it. (Or use a stick knocked against the brush.) Repeat until the whole frame is evenly covered with dots. Wipe any running dots with a cloth. Any number of colours can be spattered and a variety gives a more textured look, which gives the final finish a richer appearance – we used two layers of colour here.

Four After you've finished, give the frame one or two coats of polyurethane varnish to protect it and to help create a smooth finish – we used a high-gloss polyurethane varnish tinted with red, burnt umber, and black oil colours. A wood-coloured varnish, such as mahogany or oak, could be used instead of mixing up a coloured varnish.

Lamp Light – *Sponging a Lampbase*

You can create the most wonderful translucent, mottled effect with sponging, with colours blending into one another as they do here on this lampbase.

Sponging is particularly effective when used on small surfaces, as this lampbase proves. When we found it, it was tired-looking and old, but in working order – and easily transformed by our colour scheme.

One The lampbase to be sponged should be clean and free from grease, so wipe thoroughly with a clean rag. Give it a coat of acrylic primer, then fill in any remaining holes with an all-purpose filler. Allow the filler to dry before sanding down the surface.

Two Paint two coats of white vinyl silk emulsion or eggshell onto the lampbase and leave it to dry. We mixed I part cobalt blue with 4 parts white artists' acrylic paint, which we then added to white emulsion. (We used emulsion for the sponging layer since it dries faster than oil-based paint, allowing a faster build-up of colour.) Dab some colour onto a sponge and press it gently and lightly over the lampbase, rinsing out from time to time in water to prevent a build-up of paint. Use a dry brush to stipple the colour into any grooves that are hard to sponge so that the pattern doesn't appear broken.

Three Allow the first layer of paint to dry before mixing another shade you wish to use as a second coat – we used I part indigo blue to 4 parts white. The mottled marble effect you see here will begin to build up as more colours are applied to the base, so continue sponging until you've achieved the effect you want – we used two layers on this lampbase. Use more if you want a more dramatic effect.

Four After you've finished, give the base a coat of clear matt polyurethane varnish to protect it and to seal in the water-based colours. If you don't do this, and if you leave gouache and acrylic paints unprotected in any way, they will gradually rub away.

The Bronze Age – *Verdigris on a Chair*

True verdigris is formed when materials such as copper and bronze oxidize on exposure to the natural elements over a long period of time. Re-creating it is relatively easy and can give a particularly dramatic, aged look to quite ordinary surfaces and furniture.

A verdigris finish is an especially effective way to brighten up exposed radiators and pipes, and it looks particularly effective on metal furniture like this iron chair, which can look appealing both inside and outside the house. Although both oil- and water-based paints can be used for verdigris, if the furniture is to spend time outside, it is advisable to use oil-based paints as they are water resistant, unlike emulsion paints.

One Give the chair a coat of red oxide metal primer (this is a general metal primer).

Two You could mix your own colour but we took the easy route and bought a can of copper-coloured oil-based eggshell paint for the first layer of this chair. Apply loosely with a dry brush (unload most of the paint onto paper towels or old newspapers), so that it just catches the surface of the chair.

Three We applied two shades of ready-mixed green eggshell to the chair, allowing the first coat to dry before applying the second colour. The first coat here was an aqua (blue-green) colour, while the second was a darker, emerald green. Again, the paint should be loosely applied, only partially covering the chair so that the brown colour shows through. Sponge or stipple the paint for a natural effect – it should not look like a conventional paint finish. Thin down the aqua paint with plenty of white spirit (use water if you are working with emulsion paints) and apply a third layer. (This is to tone down the emerald green and give a dusty, dull finish to the chair.)

Four After you've finished, give the chair a coat of clear matt polyurethane varnish to protect it against wear and tear.

Art of Deception
Trompe L'œil on a Trunk

The intent of trompe l'œil *is to 'trick the eye'; it can add focus, even wit, to the most mundane object.*

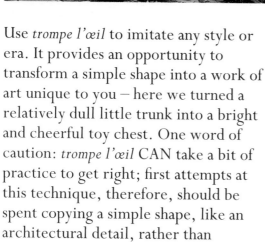

Use *trompe l'œil* to imitate any style or era. It provides an opportunity to transform a simple shape into a work of art unique to you – here we turned a relatively dull little trunk into a bright and cheerful toy chest. One word of caution: *trompe l'œil* CAN take a bit of practice to get right; first attempts at this technique, therefore, should be spent copying a simple shape, like an architectural detail, rather than something complicated.

One The piece of furniture to be painted should be clean and free from grease, so wipe thoroughly with a clean rag. Give it a coat of acrylic wood primer, then fill in any remaining holes with an all-purpose filler. Allow the filler to dry before finally sanding down the surface.

Two We chose an overall background colour of yellow ochre ready-mixed emulsion paint for the base colour (you can use either oil-based or water-based paints over acrylic wood primer). When it was dry, we applied a second coat using a warm brown water paint, I part colour to 3 parts water, dabbing it off gently with a rag.

While it was still drying, we spattered some more of the same watery paint over the surface and left it to dry.

Three Begin the *trompe l'œil* by studying the piece of moulding or other design you want to copy. See where the light falls to create shadows and break it down into three parts: highlight, midtone, and shadow. Pencil the moulding design onto the box to give yourself guidelines. Paint a test line onto a piece of paper first before you tackle the box itself. Taking your base colour as the midtone, carefully apply a line of paint with a loaded brush, using a ruler to keep the edge straight. (Don't let the edge of the ruler actually come into contact with the surface – hold it a few millimetres away.) Now quickly take another brush of about the same size loaded with water and run it down one side of the original line – the water will blend in to give a natural softening, and you will be left with a hard and a soft edge. (The secret of *trompe l'œil* is the softening of the lines.) When all the main lines have been painted on, enhance and emphasize the effect with greater control, using coloured pencils. After you've finished, give it a coat of clear matt or semi-gloss polyurethane varnish to protect it.

Four We created the freehand design within the moulding by drawing the selected subject onto a piece of paper (you could trace it if you find this easier). Transfer it onto the desired area of the trunk by tracing it or by placing the drawing over some carbon paper. Paint in the large areas of colour first, then bring out the details with smaller brushes, pencils, and pens. After you've finished, give the painting a coat of clear matt polyurethane varnish to protect it.

Window Dressing
Stencilling Around a Window

Traditionally, stencilling was used as a cheap alternative to wallpaper. These days, it is most often used to add interest to large flat areas of colour or, as here, to 'frame' and highlight a room feature, such as a window.

If you have decided to choose shutters instead of curtains for your room, stencilled patterns can be an ideal way of adding colour and interest to the window frame – without detracting from the room's simple lines. You can use the same design in any size, and create a coordinated look throughout the room by stencilling walls, doors, and fabrics to match.

One Invent a design or adapt an idea from a book or piece of material for your stencil. (You can enlarge or reduce it to the required size by photocopying it.) The pattern for this stencil was drawn up on a piece of squared paper and repeated several times. Transfer your design onto a piece of acetate or stencil card by tracing carefully. Use a scalpel or stanley knife to cut out the stencil.

Two If you are using a number of different colours for your stencil, cut out each area of colour on separate pieces of card or acetate. Ready-mixed stencil paints and sprays can be used as an alternative to emulsion, gouache, or acrylic paint. We used artists' acrylic paints mixed with white emulsion – 2 parts green to 1 part raw umber and a little yellow ochre were mixed into a 250ml (scant $\frac{1}{2}$ pint) of white emulsion for the first colour. Mark out the area around the window to be stencilled with pencil register marks.

Three Attach the stencil to the wall with masking tape or spray adhesive where you want to begin the pattern. Rub a little paint onto a stippling or stencil brush, dabbing off any excess paint so the brush is very dry. Dab the first colour onto the wall through the stencil with a slight rocking movement, ensuring that all the edges are well defined. Allow the paint to dry before removing the stencil. Move onto the next position and continue until the area has been completed. Repeat the process using the second colour – we mixed 2 parts cobalt blue to 1 part burnt umber, again mixed into 250ml (a scant $\frac{1}{2}$ pint) of white emulsion. Paint can form on the back of the stencil, which will cause smudging, so be sure to wipe it occasionally.

Four After you've finished, give the pattern a coat of clear matt polyurethane varnish to protect it. If you sand the stencil pattern lightly when it is dry, it will give it an aged quality. Or you could paint a thin dilution of white emulsion over the design to tone it down and give an appealing 'fresco' look.

Antiquing creates a sense of age, an authentic-looking discolouring and fading to suggest the passage of time. It is the perfect finish to use if you want to restore character to an old piece of furniture or embellish a new one, like these two chairs.

Old Chairs from New –
Antiquing a pair of Kitchen Chairs

Old wooden chairs can be picked up cheaply and easily from junk shops or auctions. Be careful in making your choice, however—there is a difference between looking old and looking tatty. Make sure that the basic design is pleasing and that the chairs are in good enough condition to function practically after their makeover. Antiquing can make them look authentically aged—it cannot improve their comfort rating!

One The chairs must be clean and free from grease, so wipe thoroughly with a clean rag. Give them a couple of coats of acrylic wood primer, then fill in any remaining holes with an all-purpose filler. Allow the filler to dry before finally sanding down the surface. Just before painting, run a dry brush over each chair to remove any lingering dust – a clean rag or 'tack rag' is ideal to remove any unseen particles.

Two Apply one coat of light eggshell paint to each of the chairs – we used a teaspoon of pale green oil colour mixed with 500ml (1 pint) of white eggshell on the first chair, and the same quantities, using a pale blue oil colour, on the second one – and let them dry. Duller earth colours give a more appropriate 'antique' look than stronger, bright colours. Apply a second coat of eggshell, in a darker colour; we mixed slightly darker shades of green and blue oil colour with white eggshell, using the same quantities as before. Two tones of one colour or a similar colour (as here) can be used to achieve the antiqued look, but contrasting colours would work well, too.

Three Sandpaper the paint, rubbing gently back to the base coat in some areas. Continue sanding down until you have the desired look – these chairs were only lightly sanded to give a more subtle antique look; heavy sanding will give a bolder finish.

Four After you've finished, give the chairs a coat of brown wax or dark tan boot polish. Using a rag, work the polish into any cracks and use a brush to pick up details. We used boot polish, but brown scumble glaze or dirty varnish can be used as alternatives to wax or polish.

A Polished Performance
Lacquering a Table

Faux lacquering gives a very striking finish to simple, rather uninteresting furniture — bold colours can look particularly effective but be wary of using them on large pieces where they could be a little strident.

Any surface can be lacquered though it is most effective on smooth areas, such as this small occasional table. Lacquering produces a depth and intensity of colour which does not compare with silk or gloss finishes.

One The piece of furniture to be lacquered should be clean and free from grease, so wipe thoroughly with a clean rag. Give it a coat of acrylic wood primer, then fill in any remaining holes with an all-purpose filler. Allow the filler to dry before sanding down the surface. Remove any lingering dust – a clean rag or 'tack rag' is ideal to remove any unseen particles.

Two Apply a first coat of red eggshell and leave to dry before applying a second coat.

Three Toning down strong colours will give a softer antique look to the lacquer. For this table, we mixed 3 parts crimson with 1 part black oil colour. This was thinned with white spirit and added to an oil-based glaze to the consistency of double cream. (The black helps to give it a more aged look.) Drag a thin layer of the glaze evenly all over the table to give a soft, grainy effect, blending out any hard edges with a softening brush.

Four Now paint a coat of red polish or shellac onto the table to add to the richness of the effect. (Varnish can be used as an alternative to polish.)

Five Original Japanese lacquering has great depth and richness, built up from layers and layers of carefully applied lacquer. You can achieve some of this depth and intensity at least, by giving the table several coats of clear gloss or semi-gloss polyurethane varnish. The varnish, which also helps to protect the table, should be thinned with white spirit (approximately 3 parts varnish to 2 parts white spirit).

Ways with Wood
Woodgraining a Door

Woodgraining is an effective way to improve the look of poor-quality wood or chipboard; the same 'disguise' could be given to tired skirting boards (baseboards).

Many doors, once stripped, will reveal a rather disappointing base of wood, as this one did – and in such cases, woodgraining can help lift it, with the added advantage that you can choose your own 'wood' finish to match the rest of your decor.

One Although you can paint the woodgrain effect onto an existing paint finish, if there is any old peeling paint it must be stripped off and sanded down. After sanding, scrub down the wood to make sure it is free from any traces of dirt, grease, and wax, then allow it to dry. Apply a coat of oil-based wood primer – we mixed a little yellow ochre oil into ours; mixing a little colour like this will give a richer finish.

Two Because we were woodgraining on wood, we worked with colours which resemble natural wood. For the first coat, we used 2 parts raw umber to 1 part raw sienna powder pigment. Dissolve the pigment in hot or boiling water and allow it to cool before mixing it with an emulsion glaze to the consistency of double cream (we used 1 part colour to 4 parts water to achieve our effect). A few drops of washing-up liquid will help bind it together. Study some pieces of wood to see the natural patterns and highlights, then paint the glaze evenly over the surface. Using a dry wide-bristled brush, drag the glaze over the door, to imitate the flow of natural woodgrain. The more pressure you apply to the brush, the deeper the woodgrained effect will be.

Three Next we mixed up an oil glaze tinted with the oil colours as before – the mixture should remain thick so don't add too much white spirit. (Emulsion onto emulsion can be too absorbent so we used an oil-based glaze for our second coat – it dries out less quickly and can therefore be worked longer.) Using a fine pencil brush, apply the glaze to the door, again imitating the patterns of wood. If you want a slightly curvy grain, wobble the brush slightly. Soften the patterns by gently brushing a dusting brush across the surface before the glaze has dried.

Four After you have finished, apply a coat of tinted semi-gloss polyurethane varnish to protect it from wear and tear. The varnish used here was tinted with a little yellow ochre and white oil colour, which helped tone down and blend the effect on the door.

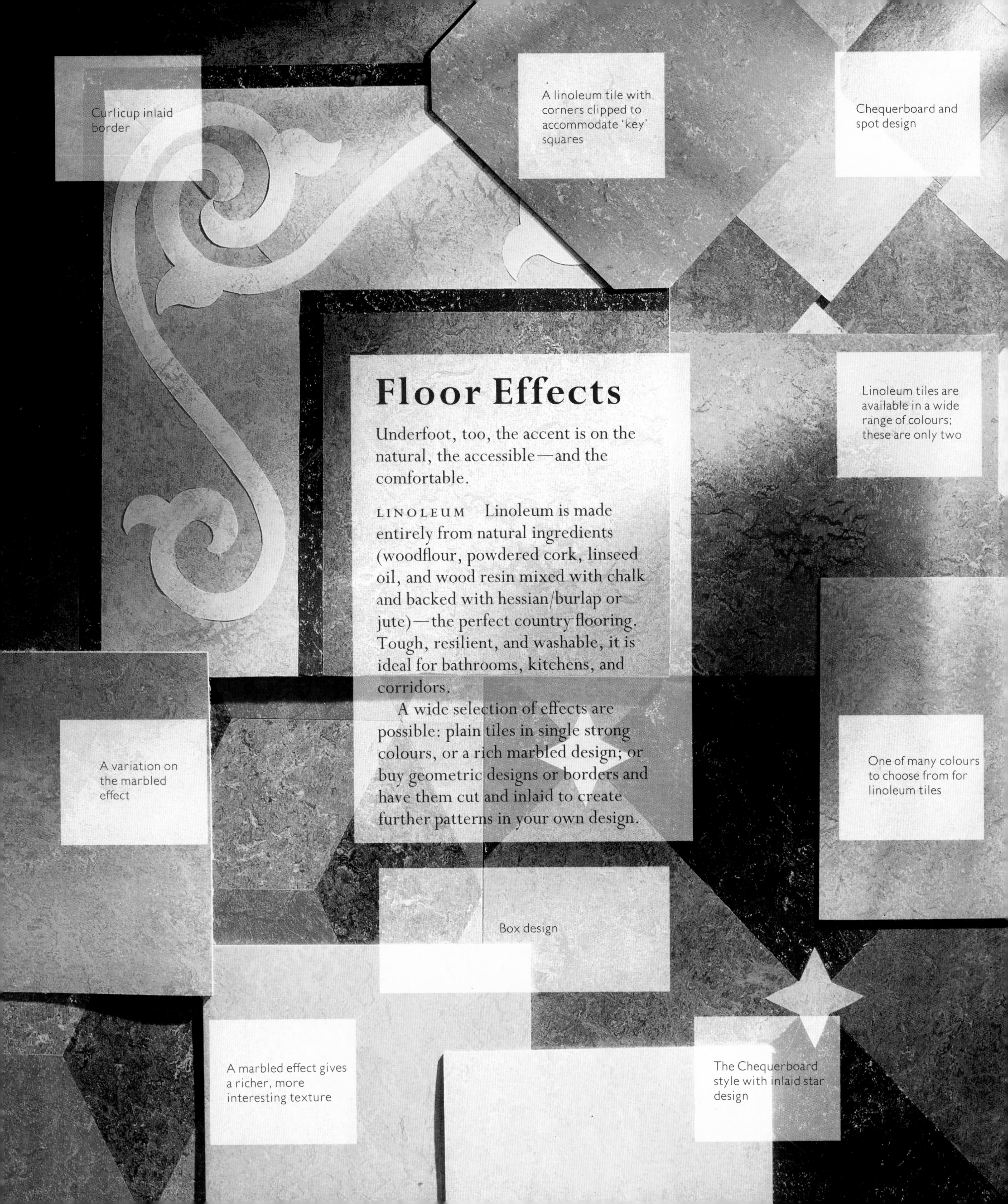

Curlicup inlaid border

A linoleum tile with corners clipped to accommodate 'key' squares

Chequerboard and spot design

Floor Effects

Underfoot, too, the accent is on the natural, the accessible—and the comfortable.

LINOLEUM   Linoleum is made entirely from natural ingredients (woodflour, powdered cork, linseed oil, and wood resin mixed with chalk and backed with hessian/burlap or jute)—the perfect country flooring. Tough, resilient, and washable, it is ideal for bathrooms, kitchens, and corridors.

A wide selection of effects are possible: plain tiles in single strong colours, or a rich marbled design; or buy geometric designs or borders and have them cut and inlaid to create further patterns in your own design.

Linoleum tiles are available in a wide range of colours; these are only two

A variation on the marbled effect

One of many colours to choose from for linoleum tiles

Box design

A marbled effect gives a richer, more interesting texture

The Chequerboard style with inlaid star design

A piece of flagstone from Peru

These Italian marble tiles can be used on their own or combined with other tiles to make subtle patterns

Encaustic tiles originate from Morocco where they are still made today

Limestone has a more refined appearance than other traditional stones

Natural stone from the Pennine Hills of England

TILE, SLATE, AND STONE   Marble, tile, and stone were the original flooring materials for country houses, and date back to Classical times when they were used with other materials in different shapes and sizes to form the earliest inlaid flooring. Today they can still create an authentic effect: terracotta or quarry tiles for a traditional bathroom floor, for instance, flagstones to add a timeless quality to a kitchen, or a marble floor to give a Mediterranean flavour to a light airy living room.

All the tiles, slates, and stones used in flooring share the same basic ingredients: earth—tiles such as terracotta, quarry, and ceramic are fired while slate and stone are naturally quarried.

Octagonal terracotta tiles provide a variation on the traditional square shape

Glazed tiles in different sizes can be used for both floors and walls

Victorian floors were often a combination of encaustic tiles, slate, and marble

A silver blue slate from Africa

A handmade terracotta tile with traditional rustic finish

Predominantly black with golden highlights, this slate comes from Africa

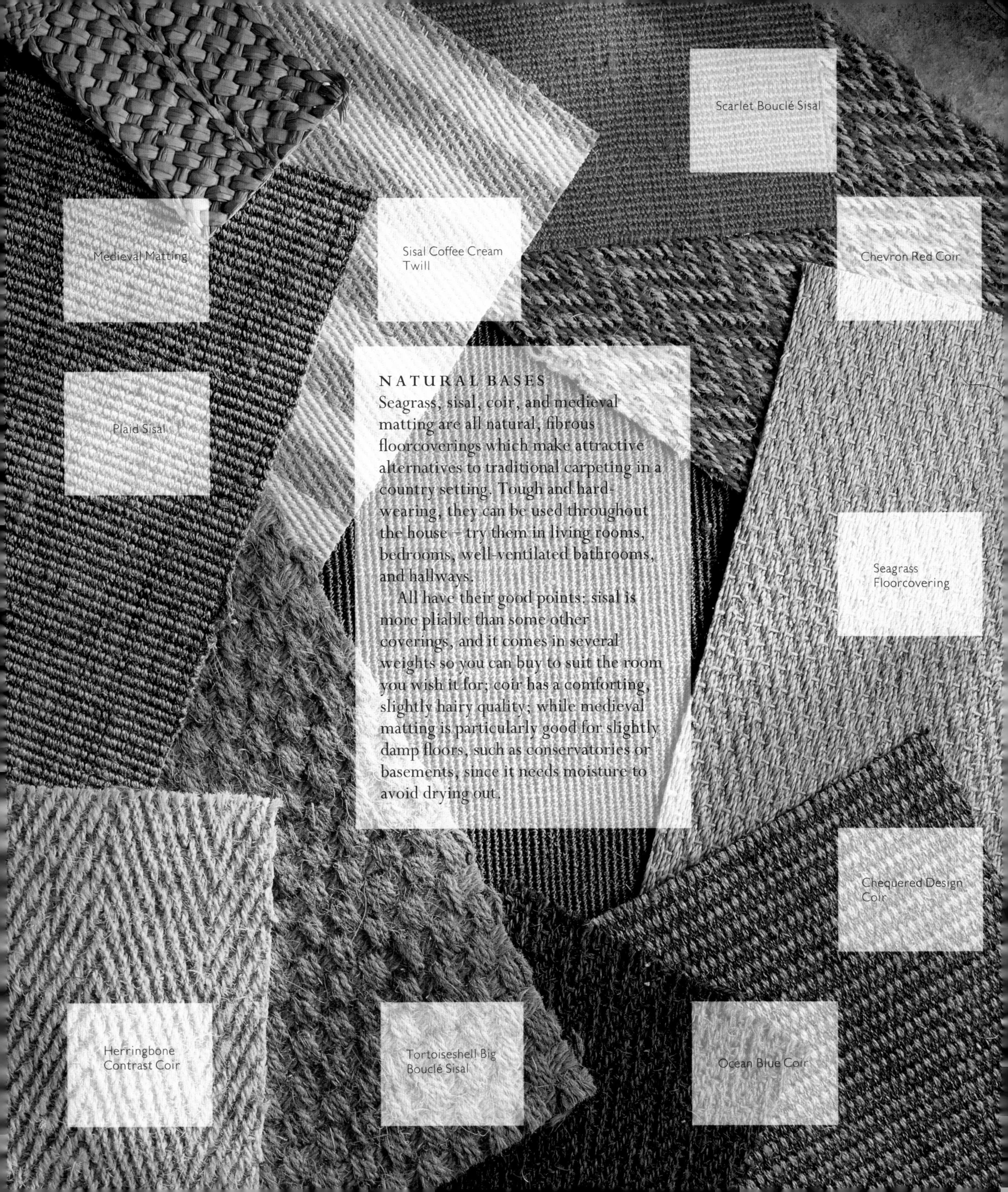

Scarlet Bouclé Sisal

Medieval Matting

Sisal Coffee Cream Twill

Chevron Red Coir

Plaid Sisal

NATURAL BASES

Seagrass, sisal, coir, and medieval matting are all natural, fibrous floorcoverings which make attractive alternatives to traditional carpeting in a country setting. Tough and hard-wearing, they can be used throughout the house – try them in living rooms, bedrooms, well-ventilated bathrooms, and hallways.

All have their good points: sisal is more pliable than some other coverings, and it comes in several weights so you can buy to suit the room you wish it for; coir has a comforting, slightly hairy quality; while medieval matting is particularly good for slightly damp floors, such as conservatories or basements, since it needs moisture to avoid drying out.

Seagrass Floorcovering

Chequered Design Coir

Herringbone Contrast Coir

Tortoiseshell Big Bouclé Sisal

Ocean Blue Coir

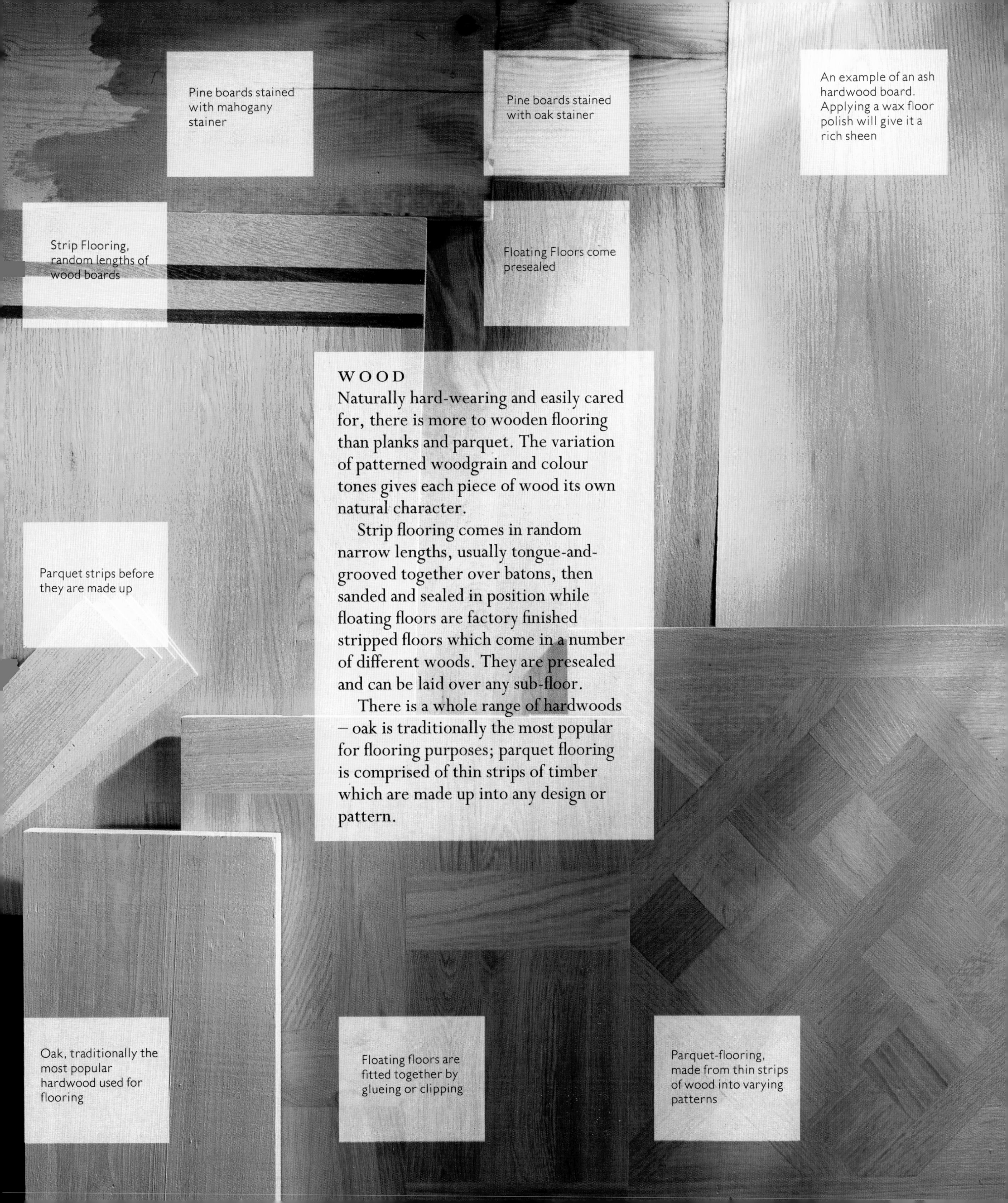

Pine boards stained
with mahogany
stainer

Pine boards stained
with oak stainer

An example of an ash
hardwood board.
Applying a wax floor
polish will give it a
rich sheen

Strip Flooring,
random lengths of
wood boards

Floating Floors come
presealed

Parquet strips before
they are made up

WOOD

Naturally hard-wearing and easily cared
for, there is more to wooden flooring
than planks and parquet. The variation
of patterned woodgrain and colour
tones gives each piece of wood its own
natural character.

Strip flooring comes in random
narrow lengths, usually tongue-and-
grooved together over batons, then
sanded and sealed in position while
floating floors are factory finished
stripped floors which come in a number
of different woods. They are presealed
and can be laid over any sub-floor.

There is a whole range of hardwoods
– oak is traditionally the most popular
for flooring purposes; parquet flooring
is comprised of thin strips of timber
which are made up into any design or
pattern.

Oak, traditionally the
most popular
hardwood used for
flooring

Floating floors are
fitted together by
glueing or clipping

Parquet-flooring,
made from thin strips
of wood into varying
patterns

A Fiery Focus
Tiling Around a Fireplace

A fireplace often seems to be the heart of a room, especially during those winter months when the natural elements are raging outdoors. Decorating the area around the fireplace can provide an elegant echo to this natural focal point — especially when a good log fire is casting its glow onto the tiles.

There is an almost limitless choice of patterned and plain tiles that would be suitable to tile around a fireplace. We used 10cm (4in) ceramic tiles to cover approximately a 75cm × 60cm (30in × 24in) area. It involved using fifty-four tiles. If you don't feel up to cutting tiles, you can use special border tiles instead.

One Mark off the area you plan to cover, then lay a 'dry run' of tiles to check the rough fit and identify any possible cutting problems. Always lay on as flat a surface as possible. If you are using non self-adhesive tiles as we did here, spread a thin layer of ceramic tile adhesive over the surface to be tiled. Now lay the tiles carefully over the adhesive, allowing even gaps between each tile for grouting. Work out from the centre of the area for the best results. When you come to the edges, use a tilecutter to cut the tiles into shape if necessary. Leave for 6 – 8 hours to allow the adhesive to 'set'. Then grout the tiles, using a thin blade to get the grout into the gaps between the tiles. (Grout is a chalky substance which helps protect the tiles against water.) Clean off any excess grout with a damp sponge. For a neater look, run the end of a wooden spoon through the gaps, which will help to pack the grout and stop it cracking. Leave to dry, then polish the tiles with a dry cloth.

Two Giving new tiles a coating of crackle varnish can lend them a timeless quality. This impression of age is further enhanced if you choose a patterned tile inspired by a traditional design, such as delft – similar to the tile used here. Oil-based crackle varnish can be bought from most paint suppliers and comprises two elements: an oil-based patinating varnish and a water-based crackle varnish. Begin by painting

the patinated varnish onto the tiles. Leave for a couple of hours or longer – the tiles should be tacky (but not completely dry). The time this will take depends on the temperature of the room.

Three Paint the crackle varnish onto the tiles. After about 20–30 minutes, as the varnish begins to dry, cracks will start to show. Use heat on the tiles if you want more pronounced cracks on your tiles. This layer of varnish should be left for about 4 hours.

Four Using a ready-mixed brown or black tile paint and a small brush, carefully paint each tile individually. Apply the paint to the tiles, then wipe it off with a rag immediately; paint will seep into the cracks and any excess will come off with the rag. After you've finished all the tiles, give them another, final, coat of patinated varnish to protect and seal them.

Chequered Footnote
Laying an Inlay Floor

Painting a floor can be a simple and dramatic way to revive tired old floorboards — and is inexpensive, especially when compared with the cost of carpeting.

The pattern for this floor follows a traditional chequerboard design, but you can adapt any pattern to suit yourself — the only constraint is your own imagination! Inlay flooring can be done using a variety of wood stainers to imitate natural wood tones — or indeed any colour combination can be used to create the effect you wish.

One Old floorboards must be prepared first before being painted; for the best results, hire a sanding machine to sand down the boards. After sanding, scrub them down to make sure that they are free from any traces of dirt, grease, and wax, then allow them to dry. Apply a coat of oil-based primer (floors take a lot of punishment and an oil-based primer will be much tougher-wearing than a water-based one).

Two Begin the inlay painting by giving the floor a coloured wash of paint — we used 2 parts raw umber mixed with 1 part raw sienna powder pigment. Dissolve the pigment in hot or boiling water and allow it to cool before mixing it with an emulsion glaze; the glaze should be the consistency of single cream. Apply the wash onto the foor, then wipe it off with a rag.

Three To create an inlay flooring like the one shown, mask off the floor into 25cm (10in) squares, using 5cm (2in) masking tape. Use a stanley knife to 'key' around the squares. We used an oil-based walnut stainer for this floor — paint the stainer onto the floor, being careful to stick to the marked squares and not let it seep past the key line of the edges. Wipe off any excess with a rag.

Four Cut out each of the 5cm (2in) squares where the tape crosses over itself. A different coloured stainer can be used for these squares — we used an oil-based deep mahogany stainer here. After you've finished, remove the remaining masking tape and give the floor two or three coats of clear matt or semi-gloss polyurethane varnish to protect it from heavy wear and tear.

First Impressions
A Floor Painted after the Style of Matisse

Be bold, brave, and adventurous — and use vibrant colours to brighten up your floor! Colourful floor designs and patterns can replace conventional rugs and carpeting in the right kind of room (like this small bedroom).

The pattern for this floor was inspired by a Matisse painting. We worked with a variety of colours using ready-mixed oil-based paints. When working on a somewhat abstract design like this floor, don't be constricted as you work – let the brush flow and paint with confidence.

One Old floorboards must be prepared first before being painted; for the best results hire a sanding machine to sand down the boards. After sanding, scrub them down to make sure they are clean and free from any traces of dirt, grease, or wax, then allow them to dry. Apply a coat of oil-based primer (floors take a lot of punishment, and an oil-based primer will be much tougher-wearing than a water-based one).

Two Begin by painting on the base colour – the most dominant colour in the design (in this case, pink). Allow the paint to dry before drawing on the design with pencils, chalk, and charcoal. We used chalk lines as a guide for the straight lines on this floor since they rub off easily afterwards.

Three Broadly paint in large areas of colour. This is a 'loose' design so don't be afraid of the paint; working wet paint into wet paint, you will be able to achieve an exciting, painterly effect. Leave to dry, then complete the design using smaller, denser brushes to bring out the finer detailing and design on the floor.

Four After you've finished, give the floor two or three coats of clear matt or semi-gloss polyurethane varnish to protect it against heavy wear and tear.

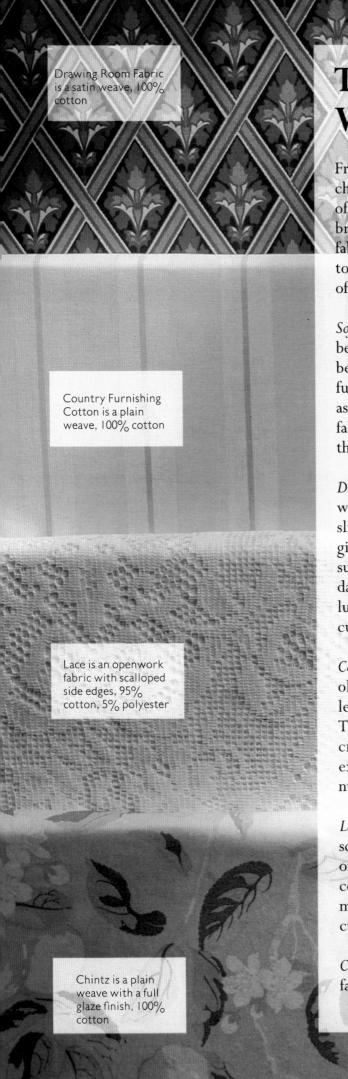

Drawing Room Fabric is a satin weave, 100% cotton

Country Furnishing Cotton is a plain weave, 100% cotton

Lace is an openwork fabric with scalloped side edges, 95% cotton, 5% polyester

Chintz is a plain weave with a full glaze finish, 100% cotton

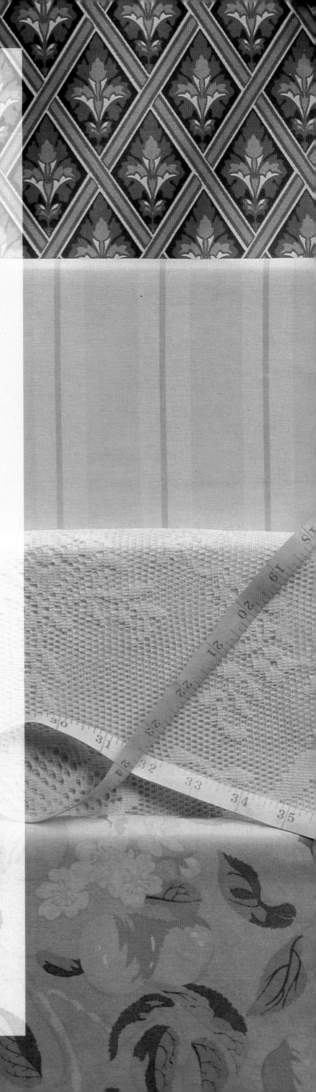

The Material World

From ticking to linen, checks to chintzes, fashions change and the range of fabrics and designs grows increasingly broad. Here we show the diversity of fabrics in the Laura Ashley Collection, to give an idea of the breadth and depth of what is available generally.

Soft furnishing or drape fabrics can be used for curtains, cushions, blinds or bedcovers – or indeed, any type of soft furnishing. They are not so hardwearing as the range known as upholstery fabrics, so it is not advisable to use them to cover sofas or chairs.

Drawing Room Fabric is a medium-weight satin-weave material with a slight sheen effect and a texture which gives rich vibrancy to warm colours, such as burgundy, and a deep glow to dark colours, such as bottle green. Its luxurious feel is effective when used as curtains or other wall-hangings.

Country Furnishing Cotton is the oldest fabric in the Collection and is less expensive than most other fabrics. The wide selection of designs on this crisp cotton gives the opportunity to experiment with new ideas for any number of fresh, light, new looks.

Lace is a fine openwork fabric with a scalloped side edge. It can be used on its own as curtains or cushions, or in conjunction with other materials to make a crisp edging for blinds, cushions, and bedcoverings.

Chintz is a lightweight plain-weave fabric with full glaze finish which, over

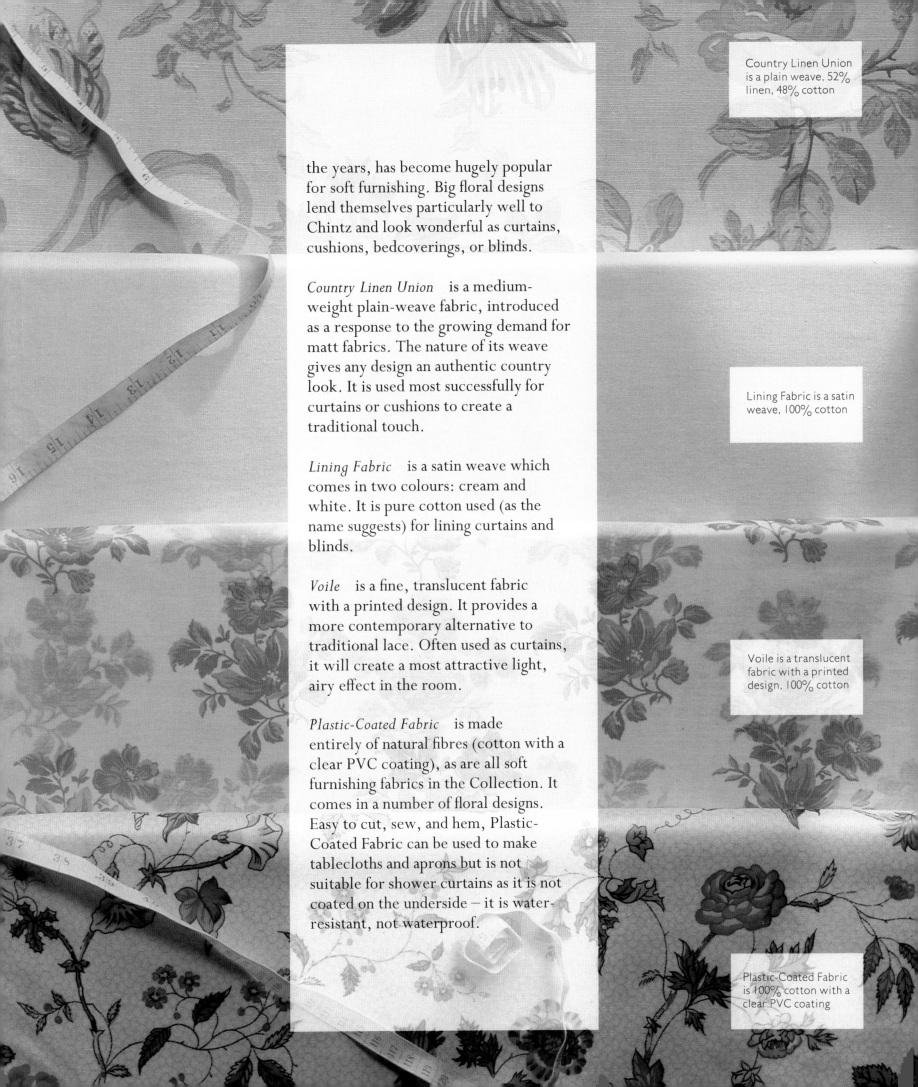

the years, has become hugely popular for soft furnishing. Big floral designs lend themselves particularly well to Chintz and look wonderful as curtains, cushions, bedcoverings, or blinds.

Country Linen Union is a medium-weight plain-weave fabric, introduced as a response to the growing demand for matt fabrics. The nature of its weave gives any design an authentic country look. It is used most successfully for curtains or cushions to create a traditional touch.

Lining Fabric is a satin weave which comes in two colours: cream and white. It is pure cotton used (as the name suggests) for lining curtains and blinds.

Voile is a fine, translucent fabric with a printed design. It provides a more contemporary alternative to traditional lace. Often used as curtains, it will create a most attractive light, airy effect in the room.

Plastic-Coated Fabric is made entirely of natural fibres (cotton with a clear PVC coating), as are all soft furnishing fabrics in the Collection. It comes in a number of floral designs. Easy to cut, sew, and hem, Plastic-Coated Fabric can be used to make tablecloths and aprons but is not suitable for shower curtains as it is not coated on the underside – it is water-resistant, not waterproof.

Country Linen Union is a plain weave, 52% linen, 48% cotton

Lining Fabric is a satin weave, 100% cotton

Voile is a translucent fabric with a printed design, 100% cotton

Plastic-Coated Fabric is 100% cotton with a clear PVC coating

Woven Check is a plain-weave fabric with a check design, 87% cotton, 13% nylon

Coloured Woven Jacquard is a figured fabric with a sprig motif

Ottoman is a plain weave with a rib effect, 100% cotton

Traditional Cotton is a plain weave, 100% cotton

UPHOLSTERY FABRICS

All of the fabrics in the Upholstery Fabric Collection are particularly hard-wearing, which makes them most suitable as sofa or chair coverings.

Woven Check is a very popular upholstery fabric. Strong influences from European countries like France and Sweden in recent years have caused an upsurge in demand for checks and stripes. They can be mixed with all types of patterned or plain designs, to complete a look in any room.

Coloured Woven Jacquard is a heavyweight figured fabric carrying a small sprig motif. Woven on a jacquard loom, it is 86% cotton and 14% nylon and is suitable for all types of upholstery. As tastes change, there has recently been increased demand for tonal textures to be used in upholstery and a decline in demand for the more traditional floral design.

Ottoman is a heavyweight plain-weave fabric with a rib effect. It is a standard upholstery fabric but can also look very effective when used as piping with another textured material.

. *Traditional Cotton* is a medium-weight plain-weave matt fabric with a textural appearance. The open weave of traditional cotton breaks up the design on the fabric so that it is more toned in appearance than, say, Country Furnishing Cotton. Traditional

Cotton is one of only two materials in the Laura Ashley Collection which can be used for both upholstery and soft furnishings.

Ticking has also become popular in recent years. A heavy-weight fabric with a herringbone weave, ticking is a cheaper upholstery fabric, which can be coordinated with all types and textures of material.

Woven Jacquard is a heavyweight figured fabric with a textured trellis design. Extremely versatile and hardwearing, its inherent woven texture adds interest to a plain colour.

Upholstery Fabric is a heavyweight plain-weave material similar in appearance to traditional cotton, although it is more textural and also more hard-wearing. As with all other Laura Ashley upholstery fabrics, it is fire retarded. Its simple appearance sits very happily with other, more highly patterned, chintzes and cottons.

Satin Weave is printed with a sophisticated floral design, which gives the effect of woven damask. It is a colour carrier and works as a subtle alternative to more obvious Chintz. Satin Weave has a matt shine but does not carry the heavy feel of damask. Like Traditional Cotton, it can be used for both upholstery and soft furnishings.

Ticking is a herringbone-weave fabric with a striped design, 100% cotton.

Woven Jacquard is 53% wool, 35% cotton, 12% nylon

Upholstery Fabric is a plain weave, 100% cotton

Satin Weave gives the effect of woven damask, 100% cotton

Decorative Details

A few quick sewing ideas for bedrooms and bathrooms

TISSUE COVERS

Tuck away your tissues in an easy-to-make fabric cover like the one below. Cut one piece of fabric 32.5cm (13in) long and fold it in half with the right sides together. Make 5cm (2in) opening in the middle of what will be the top side of the fabric. At each end of the opening, make two 5mm ($\frac{1}{4}$in) diagonal cuts – forming a y-shape. Fold back the triangles this leaves and hand sew them down. Turn the right way round.

LACE PILLOWCASES

Abandon the urge to throw away old pillowcases – resurrect them by adding a length of lace and some ribbon (right). The lace can be used as a decorative border or frill, or you could cover the pillowcase completely. To edge with ribbon and lace, unpick the

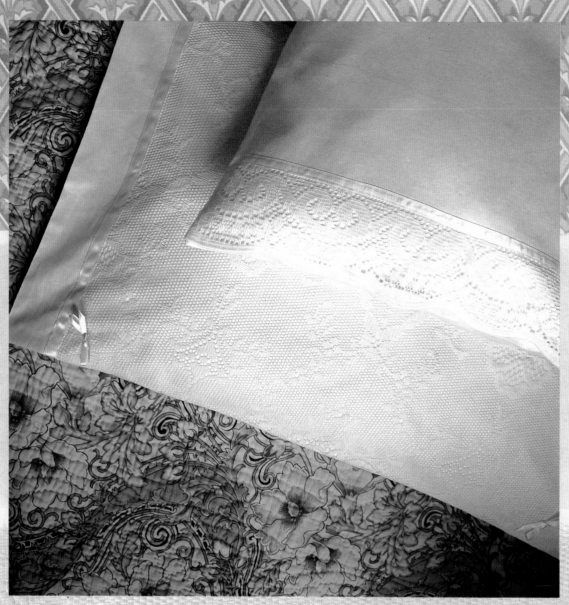

seams of the existing case and pin the lace in place to the underside of the seams. Add the ribbon, pinning it into position before sewing both into place.

LACE PILLOWCASE AND NIGHTDRESS CASE

Coordinate comfort and tidiness by using lace to make a matching pillowcase and nightdress case like those above right. To make it as we did, without using a zip, measure the dimensions of the pillow, allowing 1.5cm ($\frac{3}{4}$in) extra all round. Cut out one piece of material for the front, then another one for the back, allowing an extra 10cm (4in) for the overlap which will hold the cushion pad in place. For a frill, pin to the front piece of material,

along the stitching line. Take the back piece and fold down the overlap, right sides facing, and stitch down at the sides. Lay the front and back pieces together, right sides facing, ensuring that the frill is tucked inside, and sew the three open sides. Finally, turn the pillow case the right way out.

The nightdress case is made the same way, using a circular shape and no frill.

PIN CUSHION

Store away those endless pins and needles in a cushion which won't disappear (right). Cut out two pieces of your chosen material to the size you require. (Our dimensions were 12cm × 5cm/5in × 2in for which we needed 25cm/10in of material.) Cut out

60cm × 25cm (24in × 10in) with the right sides together. Sew a line 2.5cm (1in) from the top edge of the fabric, and another parallel line 1cm (½in) below this, leaving a 5mm (¼in) gap unsewn to pull the ribbon through.

Pin the rectangle of fabric around the base before sewing it in position. Turn in the outside edges and sew the remaining sides together. Finally, thread the ribbon or draw string. For added stability, add a base to the bag. Decide on the shape and size you want, cut out a piece of card and cover it in matching fabric.

a strip of fabric to go round the sides of the pin cushion. Sew the top onto one edge of this, and the bottom onto the other edge, leaving 2.5cm (1in) gap on the bottom side seam. Stuff with wadding through this opening, then sew up by hand. Add trimmings as you wish.

DRAW-STRING BAGS

Tidy away bedroom and bathroom necessities into bags of all shapes and sizes (far right). For a bag with a 15cm (6in) square base, you will need about 75cm (30in) of fabric. Cut out the base first, then cut a piece of fabric 60cm × 50cm (24in × 20in) to cover the circumference of the base. Allow an extra 2.5cm (1in) for hemming. Fold this material in half, so that it measures

NAPKINS

Cut out a template for the size of napkin you require and use this as a guide for all the pieces. The squares of fabric should be laid, right sides facing, and stitched, leaving a 5cm (2in) gap to pull through to the right side. Hand sew this area once pressed.

TABLECLOTH

Add interest to a plain tablecloth by adding a contrasting fringe to the edge. Pin the length around the edges of the cloth before sewing it in place. You could add detail by attaching a length of decorative ribbon above the fringe, or by adding to the cloth at the table edge.

KITCHEN CHAIR CUSHION

Measure the cushion before you cut the cover, allowing a 1.5cm (¾in) seam. Cut out material for the back, allowing an extra 10cm (4in) for the overlap which will hold the cushion in place. Fold this overlap down, right sides together, and stitch. Next, cut fabric the depth of the foam pad filling, to go around the sides as an inset. Measure around the cushion to find out how much piping you will need. Cut a strip of fabric on the cross, 5cm (2in) wide which will cover the length of piping. Cover, then pin and tack. Pin the top cover piece to the inset, right sides together, with the piping neatly inserted in the same way.

LIVING ROOM CUSHION

Add interest and detail to a simple shaped cushion by attaching braid or fringing (right). The cushion cover should be made up completely before the braid or fringe is attached. For the effect above, choose a thick braid to coordinate with the cushion cover. Place the braid around the cushion and pin it at the side edges. Then experiment for the final position. To make corner loops, as we have done, simply twist a small loop at right angles to the cushion and secure with a few stitches. Hand sew the braid in place around the cushion.

OVEN GLOVE

Liven up the kitchen by making some oven gloves from cheerful scraps of material (left). Draw around your hand generously and cut four pieces for each glove. Sandwich wadding between each set of two pieces and sew together. Then sew both wadded 'hands' together. Add a length of tape around the completed edges of the glove, pin and tack it before finally sewing in position. The tape will keep the edges tidy and give extra strength.

Quilt Edged
Making a Patchwork Throw

Patchwork is one of the most traditional of country crafts, and was, in the beginning, used to create bed-coverings. As it has become more artistic (and perhaps as central heating has reduced the necessity for heavy quilts) it is now increasingly used for a whole variety of decorative effects.

Making a patchwork quilt by hand can take literally years if the pattern is an intricate one. Here we have cheated a little by machine-stitching and by using patterned fabric to create a more intricate effect. The result is still superb, however, something you could be proud to hang on your wall, throw casually over a chair, or, as here, cover the dining room table – a real country antique in the making. Our finished quilt measured 90cm × 120cm (3ft × 4ft) and used about 9m (29ft) of fabric.

One Cut out a length of calico as a base for your quilt, a little larger than the finished size to allow for hemming (we cut to 101cm × 132cm, 40in × 52in). Work out your chosen design on a piece of paper then draw it carefully onto the calico, using a dark marker pen. Cut out a piece of fabric to act as background to the exact size of the finished quilt. Place it over the calico base, trace the design onto it and number all the sections of the design. Then cut out the pattern into the individually numbered pieces.

Two Choose a selection of fabrics to make up the quilt – try to build up a good balance of colour, working from the centre of the design. Using the numbered pieces as an outline, cut the fabrics out to size; they should be cut a little larger than required to allow the edges to be turned under. Pin the fabric pieces to the calico base. Start pinning from the central squares, working out until you reach the border. Pin the borders last.

Three As with the pinning, sew the central squares together first. The border fabrics can be added to the base after the central panel has been stitched together. Turn in the inside edges of the border fabrics before sewing to the base.

Four A length of material is needed for the back of the quilt. This should be cut to the same size as the base. To attach the front and back of the patchwork, pin the wrong sides to face each other (using the marked edges of the base as a guide) and sew around three edges. Trim off excess material. Finally, turn the quilt out the right way and stitch the remaining edge.

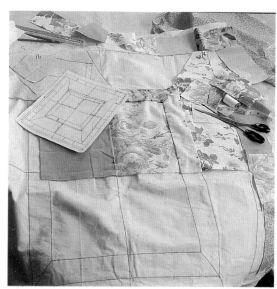

Colourful Cushions
Two Appliqué Designs

Appliqué (the craft of sewing one fabric onto another) is one of the most original ways to use scraps of material – as you can see.

GOING ROUND IN CIRCLES

Small pieces of fabric are combined here to surround a larger piece – and in so doing give texture to the final finish. This looks particularly effective on a circular cushion, but the principle could be adapted to virtually any attractive shape.

One Cut out a large circle of material for the front base of the cushion. Always cut out more material than is needed to allow the edges to be turned in. Choosing four or five different fabrics, cut out a number of small circles to go around the larger one. Arrange these approximately 5mm ($\frac{1}{4}$in) in from the edge of the large circle, overlapping each one by 1cm ($\frac{1}{2}$in). Pin them before sewing to the base with a zigzag stitch.

Two Cut out another large circle for the back of the cushion. (This can be cut out in two semi-circular halves to allow for an opening at the back where the filler or cushion is to be inserted.) Turn under and stitch the straight edge of each semi-circle to give a neater finish to the opening.

Three Cut a length of fabric (the circumference of the circle) to use as an inset strip around the cushion. (This will give it more shape.) Turn under the edges of the inset strip and the front appliqué circle, and sew them together. Pin the back of the cushion to the inset strip and attach in the same way. Turn the right way round and fill with a cushion pad.

THE FELINE FRONT

This traditional black cat is a favourite appliqué design and is used here as one simple image. It can, however, be adapted to create a collage effect, as can most appliqué subjects. (To do this, cut a variety of patterns and shapes from different fabrics and sew them onto another background material.)

One Cut out the background fabric into a square. Draw up a central square within this one, then draw a border around the edge. (For the border on this cushion, two sides and the corners were divided into squares and the remaining two sides into rectangles.) Cut out the fabric for the central square and border – these should all be about 2.5cm (1in) larger than the actual size you need, to allow for the edges to be turned in. Pin and sew together the fabrics for each side of the border so that you have a square frame.

Two Copy the outline of a cat onto a piece of paper. Cut it out and use this as an outline to cut your chosen fabric into a cat shape. Attach the cat onto the central square, using fabric glue. Zigzag stitch around the edge of the cat to give it a more defined outline. Turn in and stitch the edges of the central square and border. Sew the central square and then the border onto the background square. Use the drawn lines as a guide when attaching the border.

Three Finally, cut out the material for the back of the cushion. (This can be cut in two halves, to allow for an opening at the back. Hem the edges of each piece.) To sew back and front together, put the right sides of the fabric together and sew all the way around. Using the back opening, turn the cover through to the correct side and sew around the sides again for a firmer, sharper edge.

Creations with Contrast

Make yourself a bag for holding all your bits and pieces – and with any spare material left over, turn your hand to a stylish but simple-to-make cushion.

CRAFTY HOLD-ALL

Since crafts themselves were discovered, a simple bag has been essential to hold necessary tools and materials. This bag is easy to make and will safely store all you'll need to carry out your favourite project.

One The simplest shape for the bag is a large square. To make it durable, it will need an interlining. Cut two squares of hard-wearing calico or canvas to the required size (the bag pictured here used 50cm/20in). Leave an extra 7.5cm (3in) for a 'neck' at the top – this overlap will be where the handles are attached.

Two Next cut out two pieces of fabric, one for the front and one for the back – these should be a little smaller than the calico, about 42.5cm/17in square. Centre and stitch one piece of fabric onto each piece of calico.

Three Cut out two pieces of lining fabric to the same size as the calico, but without allowing for a neck. Sew the sides of the lining together, then sew one of the top edges to each piece of calico. Handles similar to those in the picture can be found in a variety of sizes from most craft shops. To attach them to the bag, turn the 'neck' of the calico down over the handles and sew it onto the inside of the bag to keep them in place.

Four Attach the sides of the bag together by putting the fabrics' right sides together, inside out, and sew the sides and bottom edges together. While you are sewing, let the lining hang out from the top. Sew the bottom edges on the lining, then turn the bag the right way round. If necessary, you can stitch around the edges of the bag on the right side to give a firmer, more secured edge.

CUSHION YOURSELF

A design for a cushion can be inspired by any number of sources – the simplest patterns are often the most striking. The rectangular cushion here, combining four squares and a border length of fabric, reflects the beginnings of a patchwork.

One Cut out a rectangular piece of fabric to the size of cushion you require. Draw out your design onto this piece of fabric – dividing it into four equal squares with a border on one side if you wish to follow the design here. Choose cover fabrics that will work well together and cut them to the required size and shape of your squares and border. Sew each pair of squares together, then join all four. Turn under both outside and inside edges of the border fabric and attach it along one side of the squares. Make three buttonholes, spacing them evenly along the border panel.

Two Select a fabric to use as the back of the cushion and cut it out, about one and a half times larger than the size of cushion you are making. Fold over the extra length of fabric to use as an overlap behind the border panel. Attach three buttons to this overlap in position to match the buttonholes on the front border.

Three Turn the sides of the cushions so that right sides are facing in and sew them together, about 5mm ($\frac{1}{4}$in) from the edge of the fabric. Stitch three sides of the cushion and leave the buttonholed edge open for the pad or filler. Finally, turn the cushion out the right way. Fill it with cushion pad and do up the buttons.

The traditional craft of rag rugmaking has existed for more than 200 years, and is still as satisfying and convenient a way to use up leftover fabrics as it was when it was first developed.

Something from Scraps— *Making a rug from rags*

Any odd pieces can go into your rug, but it is best to have material of a similar weight and to avoid fabrics with an open weave. A rug of 120cm × 75cm (4ft × 2½ft), similar to that shown in the photograph, will need about 18m (58ft) of fabric: 12m (39ft) of a base colour and 2–3m (6½–9¾ft) of each of the contrasting fabrics. Cut the material to 2.5cm (1in) in width, leaving it as long as possible.

One Use hessian (burlap) as a base and cut it to 5cm (2in) wider all round than the rug itself will be, to allow for hemming and shrinkage. Double-fold the edges of the hessian (burlap) and zigzag carefully on a machine, making sure the corners are very well secured.

Two Try to draw inspiration from your surroundings when you create the pattern for your rug. Drawing the design on a grid system can make it easier to work out the different areas of colour accurately. Then transfer the pattern onto the hessian using a thick marker pen. Start working from the middle of the

pattern, gradually moving outwards. With this rag rug, the inner circles were worked on first, moving out to the flowers and finally the outer circles. The areas between the flowers were done last of all.

Three Using a 'proddy' tool (a hook-like instrument), push the first end of material through the hessian (burlap), working from the back and leaving about 2.5cm (1in) on the other side. Leave about 4 spaces in the weave, and push through a loop of material, again leaving about 2.5cm (1in) on the other side. Continue like this until the length of material finishes. Begin a new length in the last hole used. Continue following the pattern until the hessian (burlap) is full. At this stage, the loops can be cut and trimmed which will give the rug a shaggy, pile effect. Or you may prefer to leave the loops uncut.

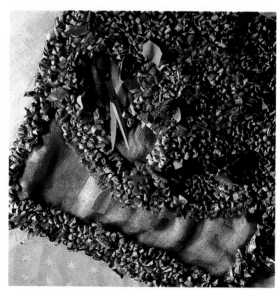

Fire Highlighter – *Creating a Firescreen from Scraps of Fabric*

Rugs are not the only thing that can be made from fabric scraps – using the same technique, wall hangings and even screens (as here) can easily be run up. And the resulting 'sampler' creates a different and unusual focal point for your fireplace.

The fish design we used in this firescreen involves the same technique as our rug, but since the pattern and area to be covered are smaller, we have used finer fabrics, worked more closely together. Our design measured about 60cm × 62cm (24in × 25in) and used about 8m (26ft) of fabric – about 2m (6½ft) divided between two colours for the fish and 6m (19½ft) divided among three colours for the abstract background.

One Cut all of the fabric to be used in the design to a 1cm (½in) width, leaving it as long as possible. Working with a number of different fabrics, as we did here, gives a more interesting textured surface to the collage.

Two Use hessian (burlap) as a base, and cut it 5cm (2in) wider all round than the screen itself will be, to allow for hemming and shrinkage. Double-fold the edges of the hessian (burlap) and hem with a machine, or handstitch, making sure the corners are secured. Draw your design freehand or sketch out on a grid system to work out the different areas of colour. Transfer the pattern onto the hessian (burlap).

Three Begin by working on the fish with an outline colour. Using a 'proddy' tool (a hook-like instrument), push the first end of material through the hessian (burlap), working from the back and leaving about 2cm (¾in) on the other side. Leave two spaces in the weave, and push through a loop of material, catching from the front side and again leaving about 2cm (¾in). Continue like this until the length of material is used up. Begin a new length in the last hole used. Continue as above until you have completed the outline colour of the fish; then fill in the rest of the body with the next colour. Work on the spiral centre next, using the palest colours first and working out in a circular motion towards the fish. Outline the fish, then continue working towards the border. The loops at the front of this screen were trimmed very short but you can leave them uncut.

Accessorizing Country Style

A Sense of Nature   148

Flowers for all Seasons   154

Five Minute Ideas   158

Flowers Without the Frills   162

A Christmas Welcome   164

A Wreath for all Seasons   166

Spring Bulbs for Winter Days   168

Free from the Woods and Hedgerows   170

A Handful of Herbs   172

Roses, Roses all the Way   174

Sweet Lavender, Fragrance of
     Forgotten Things   176

A Traditional Pot Pourri   178

Six Modern Pot Pourris   180

Clever Centrepieces   182

Festive Centrepieces   184

Country Collections   186

Casual Collections   188

Displays on the Level   190

Wall Displays   192

Shelves that Work   194

Self Contained   196

Outdoor Organization   198

A Sense of Nature

Few of us actually need to live in the country to earn a living these days, so our reasons for being there, or wishing to be there, are caught up with other needs: a craving for a simpler, purer existence, perhaps, a longing to return to nature and to a life bound up by passing seasons and rhythms.

To stressed, overworked city dwellers living in noisy and polluted conditions, the benefits of living in the country always seem to outweigh the difficulties. Not for them the realities of mud- or snow-blocked roads and the back-breaking task of caring for demanding animals day in and day out, the endless battle involved in keeping yourself warm in winter and the soil moist and watered in summer – their folk memory is of endless green fields and cool woods, pure air and open skies, and endless space all around.

They are right – for the pleasures of living in the country ARE real enough, AND simple enough. Fires burning scented fruitwood on the long winter nights with warm shadowy light from candles and old-fashioned lamps; a rug tucked cosily around your feet as you curl up in a saggy but comfortable armchair, perhaps planning next summer's flower garden from a choice of seed catalogues. And if you've had the foresight and been hedgerow-foraging in autumn, a glass of tingling,

Above The pleasure of collecting produce from your own garden never diminishes, and the feeling of achievement the sight of fresh beautiful things to eat, or just gloat over, brings, is perennially rewarding.

Left The simplest things can be the basis of a wonderfully colourful display. Before peppers and pears are whisked away to the kitchen to eat, enjoy them in a different way.

warming wild fruit liqueur by your side. . . . Spring and summer pleasures include picking flowers to fill the now redundant fireplaces in every room, or harvesting a salad of leaves and herbs from the kitchen garden. And there are dogs to walk and children to amuse with picnics and expeditions.

The essence of all country style is that it is simple, often spontaneous, and only takes time and effort if that is what

you have planned and wish. Hours spent lovingly stitching a patchwork quilt or petit-point cushion, for instance, or a small gardening task happily extended to fill up all the long sunlight hours of a summer's day, a piece of wooden furniture carefully buffed to mirror-like shine with home-made polish scented with lavender from your own garden – these are all tasks to be savoured, along with the small instant pleasures that country life can bring: a child's posy gathered on a spring walk and casually arranged in a jar or vase, a few flower heads floating in water to transform a tea table, some chillies strung up around the kitchen, at first decorative, then fulfilling their practical purpose in stews and spicy dips.

It is from the countryside outside the house that many of the special qualities of the style indoors comes. Nature provides the wood from which the furniture is made, and the inspiration for many of the patterns that adorn the cottons and chintzes that cover windows and chairs – and from the garden and the hedgerows come the flowers and plants that decorate and scent all of the rooms of the house. A few hours spent sowing some seeds in spring is amply rewarded throughout the rest of the year if you have flowers to pick regularly and to preserve in many different ways for later. Nor will the uncultivated land around your house let you down – regular walks in the woods and along the hedgerows at just the right time will fill baskets with free provender from edible funghi to nuts and berries, as well as contributing decorative materials to make into 'found' collections or arrangements.

When you can't grow plants outdoors, you can cultivate them indoors. Traditionally nearly every cottage window, however small, had windowsills bursting with plants taking advantage of the warmth inside and trying to catch what light they could from outside. Geraniums were a favourite, then as now, with their simple bright flowers and spicy, scented leaves, as were uncomplicated plants with cosy names like busy lizzie and mind-your-own-business. Today you can use your garden to supplement your supply of plants for your home: lift and pot some growing primroses and violets in the spring so that they can cheer your rooms with their colour and scent for a few days; through the autumn months plant bowls of mossy hyacinths and jonquils and leave them to wait in a potting shed or dark cupboard until they are ready to be brought out to create a burst of flower and fragrance during deep winter days.

Above A miniature posy of deep purple fresh lavender is tied with a gauzy ribbon to put among freshly laundered linen or stored clothes in a cupboard.

Right The silvery seedheads of old man's beard or wild clematis are a familiar sight in winter hedgerows. Another name for this plant is travellers' joy, which confirms how decorative it is indoors or out.

A GARDEN FOR ALL PURPOSES

A country garden can be however you want it to be. It does not have to be a 'cottage' garden whether you live in a cottage or not. It above all should be a place that you enjoy being in when you choose to be, and enjoy looking at from indoors for the rest of the time. How

you organize the space in it and what you plant and grow there will always depend to a great extent on its location and soil type, as well as the time you have available to care for it. But with minimal planning and effort you can create a cycle of growing and harvesting that will ensure a supply of blossoms and plants for most of the year. Any work you do will be more than rewarded, for plants and flowers in their habitat are one of the great joys of country living, and a regular supply of newly plucked fresh blooms to decorate the house another. If you have a productive garden, there are many ways in which you can use and preserve any overabundance it may give – flowers and petals not used for decoration when they are fresh can be picked and dried on the stem or as heads or petals, for instance, or pressed flat to decorate a card or form a collage. And they can be mixed with fragrances and spices later to make pot pourris, or made into lotions, preserves, and sachets to fill up and scent your store cupboards.

Herbs are another important part of country tradition that with their beauty, fragrance, and usefulness echo the major themes of the country way. You can grow herbs for anything: they have always been used to heal and to

flavour as well as to decorate. While they are best used freshly picked from the garden, surpluses can be dried or frozen successfully to provide a ready supply throughout the year. They fall into many categories, each requiring slightly different care and attention, depending on whether they are shrubby, greyish-leaved perennial types thriving in sun or well-drained soil (sage and lavender), fast-growing leafy annuals which relish moist rich soil (basil and dill), or low-growing creepers, perfect for scenting garden walkways (thyme). The ancient bay plant outgrows them all and is perfect for planting in tubs or it can become a large shady garden tree given the right conditions. None is difficult to grow; all will guarantee years of harvesting.

Since usefulness and practicality are such basics of this way of life, a true country garden should probably have at least a few vegetables or fruits; for eating raw, or for cooking, to use as centrepieces for the country table – what could be more evocative of country style than a bowl of fruit or a platter of vegetables on well-scrubbed pine? These necessities can provide just as interesting focal points for kitchens, living rooms, and dining rooms as more conventional floral ones. And there is simply nothing more satisfying or delicious than eating food from your own garden only hours after it has been gathered.

Above An autumn walk can produce an interesting pocketful from the hedges. It is fun to identify things later, and to use the harvest to decorate, to eat, or to sow a new tree.

Left A bookcase packed with books, but pressed into use as a display for other collections of a more frivolous kind, which threaten quite soon to fill every shelf completely.

NATURAL DISPLAYS AND COLLECTIONS

Making collections of permanent things such as souvenirs, framed pictures, and jugs has long been a country pastime. The things themselves may have been quite humble but not without importance in what was often a sparsely furnished and simple interior. Jugs and cups, for instance, rather than being put away, might have been hung from hooks below a dresser shelf; and the bedroom could have become the repository for precious personal collections, safe from the hurly-burly of the downstairs rooms.

Other 'finishing touches' can be equally in tune with practical living. The 'problem' of storage, for instance, largely disappears if you utilize your space imaginatively – big loose local baskets to hold vegetables and fruit perhaps (still as practical and sensible a way to store produce as has ever been devised) and sturdy, more solid ones for logs; strings of onions or garlic to provide not only tidy storage for these vegetables but instant and appropriate decorations for the kitchen as well; and clothes such as hats and boots, stored accessibly in a row on sturdy pegs or on a stand, a statement of style in themselves. A shallow basket taken on a woodland or hedgerow walk and filled with pebbles, leaves, and twigs provides not only a memento of a pleasant afternoon but an interesting collage for a cottage room.

In the pages that follow, there are many easy, inexpensive, and interesting ideas to help you preserve that country feeling, whether you are in the midst of a rural environment or an urban one. They are all faithful to the 'country' way of doing things, founded on centuries of wisdom, thrift, and need, and with a respect for materials and the intrinsic value of what is around us. It is a way worth following.

Flowers for all Seasons

The fewer preconceptions you have about how to put things together the better, if you are aiming for a natural country look. Traditionally, country arrangements were composed of flowers found wild or carefully cultivated in a precious patch of garden created specially for the purpose. So it is still. And no matter how busy your life, there should always be time to pick a handful of whatever flower is in perfect bloom to put into the nearest jug and proudly display on kitchen tables, windowsills or church altars. The words 'country flowers' conjure up all the simple varieties – cornfield poppies and chamomile, deep blue cornflowers and fat, cabbagy roses. Scent was always important and still should be. If you have a choice of what to grow, always go for the variety with a good scent and avoid modern hybrids. For cutting, grow the following: roses, of course, and annuals such as sweet peas, love-in-a-mist, marigolds, godetia, larkspurs, and helianthus as well as biennials like sweet williams, stocks, canterbury bells, and wallflowers. Bulbs such as daffodils and tulips are fine in water but you may prefer not to empty the garden of such precious blooms. Cultivate a few shrubs, too, like lilac, forsythia, viburnums and philadelphus.

Pick flowers from the garden very early in the day, before the dew has dried, or late in the evening. Give stems a drink for a few hours if possible before putting them into an arrangement. Get rid of any leaves from stems that will be below water level in the arrangement – this will prolong the life of the flowers a little.

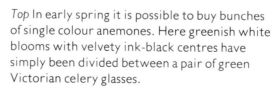

Top In early spring it is possible to buy bunches of single colour anemones. Here greenish white blooms with velvety ink-black centres have simply been divided between a pair of green Victorian celery glasses.

Above For a few brief weeks each year, pungent branches of sunny mimosa are in season. Always evocative of warm climates and scented exotic locations, the fluffy yellow flowers among deep green foliage have a magical effect on any room.

Top A humble blue-and-white striped pudding bowl has just the right character to stand up to a blazing golden yellow mass of daffodils. Invariably these simple flowers look at their best arranged by themselves and in great quantity for the most dazzling display.

Above Porcelain-pale tulips fill a generous blue-and-white pitcher and alongside are the first deep blue hyacinths in more matching china. A group of containers always looks effective.

Country flowers should never look too grand. Choose straightforward containers and flowers that you've picked for their simple charm, and combine the two with the minimum of fuss and mechanics to enjoy the results at any time of year.

Top Perfect garden roses hold the very essence of summer in their petals. Massed together in this way in an unusual metal painted trug, each colour offsets another and creates a rich glowing texture. Put the stems in damp foam or stand in water in a container inside the trug.

Above Old-fashioned shrub roses have a wonderful range of soft and subtle colours among them. They are best picked and placed simply in a sturdy mug or jar as here.

Top Flower borders in high summer are full of deep pinks, reds, blues, and purples. This French enamel jug full of blooms has the feel of a brimming herbaceous border with its rich pink scented lilies, larkspur, roses, scabious, and the small thistle-like flowers of eryngium.

Above Pearly white Iceberg roses are one of the most prolific white varieties and need nothing added to them, yet manage to look ravishing in an old blue-spattered enamel wash jug.

Top Strong yellows are difficult colours to use successfully but they are irresistible in the way they bring a splash of sunshine to their surroundings, however gloomy. A plain white jug cools down these hot rudbeckia; other pastel-coloured jugs would be effective, too.

Above Few people can resist the charm and combination of blue and white decorated china and purplish blue and white flowers. A touch of yellow really brings the contrasts alive.

Accessorizing the Country Look 155

Top Autumn is the time of year to make the most of everything decorative that isn't in flower. There are all kinds of fruits and vegetables worth displaying, such as these ornamental chillies that you can dry later to use in winter arrangements.

Above An old tin hatbox painted a rich blue-green inside is put to good use as a container for sprays of golden chillies and white snowberries. Push them into damp foam inside the box base to anchor them firmly.

Top Globe artichokes will grow prolifically enough in your kitchen garden. Leave them to open out into gorgeous mauve thistle flowers and simply display them in a shallow basket.

Above Make surplus squashes and pumpkins into flower containers by slicing off their tops and scooping out some flesh, then fill with water and put in some cheerful flowers. In summer, use watermelons in the same way, perhaps with dramatic lilies; in winter, hollowed-out apples make smaller, cosier receptacles.

Top The rich strong decoration on this early nineteenth-century porcelain teacup perfectly complements the velvety colours of poppy petals, *cosmos atrosanguineus*, and the drooping flowers of old-fashioned fuchsias.

Above A harvest collection of fruits and flowers hardly needs to be arranged any more than this. Display them as a group on an antique china plate, polished pewter, or a worn wooden board and use as an almost instant table centrepiece.

There is less to find in the garden to pick and bring indoors in winter but every flower, leaf or berry is more precious than its summer counterpart.

Top When it seems that all flowers have finished blooming for the year *nerine bowdenii* bursts into extravagant, shocking pink bloom. In a sunny well-drained part of the garden it increases over the years and makes a long-lived cut flower, always best displayed alone.

Above The mysterious branches and berries of mistletoe have a strange fascination. Seen here in silhouette against frosted glass, they have a beauty that is often overlooked. The Victorian jug just had to be used for this arrangement.

Top If you have to buy flowers during winter it is often better to choose growing flowering plants which will last for several weeks than short-lived cut flowers. Simple white primulas are pure and stylish in a split beech basket.

Above The fluffy, ghostly seed-heads of wild clematis stay in the hedgerows for most of the winter, and there are often enough of them bleached and scoured by the weather worth picking to make wonderful earthy arrangements.

Top If you have pot-grown topiary outdoors it won't hurt to bring it indoors for a short time to decorate and enjoy. Here a fat round box tree has been embellished with cranberries and tiny crab apples stuck onto short stub wires.

Above A few precious ranunculus and scented freesia are displayed among variegated foliage in a small turquoise jug. First make a posy in your hands of all the materials, then simply drop it into a suitable container and put it somewhere that invites a closer look.

Right In autumn the fruits available are so abundant and beautiful that it is a pleasure just to display them simply together with a few coloured leaves. The scents and colours are pure delight. Here there are quinces, apples, medlars, and a shiny red pomegranate.

Below Even the most prosaic of root vegetables can be seen in a new light when combined with the unexpected. Here, greeny white turnips are decorated with tiny posies of pink primroses in a pink and green sponged lustre bowl.

Above Smooth red real plums and tamarillos mingle in camouflage with a bowlful of carved wooden painted fruits. This is a useful idea to copy with other materials.

Five Minute Ideas

Small touches to a room such as flowers or arrangements of fruit or pretty natural objects can be what gives a house its life and vitality. They need not be complicated ideas which take hours to do and demand lists of materials to execute, but instead quick and simple colourful things that take just a few minutes to put together.

A bowl of fruit or a tiny posy of garden flowers are the kind of small but thoughtful touches which appear in a country interior almost without forethought. The fruit might be on its way from orchard to pantry or preserving jar and the posy a collection of a few stems of flowers from a treasured plant or scented herb. These simple ideas are perfect calendars of the season and day-to-day events, and should be as natural and understated as possible so that they simply settle in among the rest of the house. They should never look self-conscious or artificial and in time you will find that it

Below Golden-red chillies on a string hang over a chubby angel shelf; persimmons and a chilli pepper stand cheekily above. A short-lived arrangement but fun while it lasts.

Above A beloved animal portrait is crowned by a little circlet of dried berries. Made when they were fresh, the sprigs of *pyracantha* were simply wired onto a ring and allowed to dry naturally.

becomes second nature to spend a few minutes displaying something on a special plate or filling a normally empty box with a few well chosen treasures. If the idea is quick to do then it can be easily redone once the flowers are finished, or the fruit demands to be eaten.

Above Spicily hot chillies are incredibly decorative, but take care threading them and handling them even once dried, as the fiery heat can still burn eyes and skin. Piled into a shallow basket they glow with the warmth of summer sunshine.

Above During late summer there are always fruits of one sort or another ripening off on windowsills and around the kitchen. Make the most of their decorative potential while you wait for them to be ready to eat or to cook.

Below If you use large quantities of candles, you will need to store spares efficiently. They are very decorative tied into bundles of the same size and type, and good looking enough to display and not hide away.

Above A child's-size bunch of primroses tied with linen tape would make the sweetest gift. To keep the flowers fresh longer, wrap the stems in wet moss.

Right Fat, multi-petalled *ranunculus* look best used alone, either in single or mixed colours. They seem not to need green foliage to dilute their intense, deep colours. A rich taffeta bow completes a perfectly luxurious posy.

Above Scraps of fabric waiting to be used as patchwork or collections of napkins and small pieces of material look good stacked into a square or oblong basket. A practical, decorative way to store potentially messy things.

Below There are never matches where you want them and when you want them. A collection of coloured ones fills an old French match box which has seen better days, but is revived by this treatment and is useful once again.

Above In early spring the flowers of jasmine can scent a whole room. One of the best house plants and easy to keep from year to year, it is displayed here in an old lidded basket.

Above More gleanings from the roadside displayed inside a black metal money box. Old boxes and tins with compartments inside them make excellent places to display small treasures, such as pretty seeds or berries.

Above Kitchen spices and flavourings are sometimes decorative in their own right. A twig basket holds homespun cloth and little bundles of liquorice sticks, vanilla pods, and cinnamon bark scrolls.

Below A matching pair of beribboned terracotta pots hold deep cerise dried roses packed tightly together over a foam base. The rich texture of the petals needs nothing else with them which might dilute the intense colour.

Below Dried roses have been arranged in a homely cream jug just as if they were fresh ones. The mix of different colours here echoes the flower motif in the wallpaper behind, and makes the flowers look bright and lovely.

Below A cloud of pale mauve Michaelmas daisies like a Manet flower painting look best simply filling an old painted flower basket. The stems have been stood in an inner container filled with water.

Flowers Without the Frills

Decorating with flowers is simple when you understand a few basics about putting colours and shapes together, choosing the right containers, and fitting flowers to their surroundings. And fabric or wallpaper in a room can be just the starting point to lead you to make a decision about the colour or type of flowers to use. Obviously, sometimes you will begin with the flowers then find the right location for them, but starting the other way round means that you can match or contrast flower colours or types, or pick up inspiration from the feel of a fabric, or a piece of furniture.

Below An inspiration to make a garland, a posy, or anything that you can dream up from some twining stems and hedgerow berries. Sometimes the collected materials become a pleasing arrangement in themselves.

Below A sophisticated plaid fabric is the basis for a colourful vase filled with fat round *ranunculus*, which curve and bend as they please. Pink and yellow work surprisingly well together especially with green added in.

Below Country flowers can still look sophisticated when the occasion warrants it. Tulips always add glamour, even here arranged neatly into a little rustic basket standing on an elegant painted chair.

You won't need a very large number of different containers for displays of this type, although it's fun to build up a collection from fête stalls, junk shops, garage sales, or wherever you see a bargain. Baskets are one of the most useful containers for country flowers and unless they have a lovely genuine age patina (which should never be spoilt), they can always be revamped with paint or an ink stain. And don't despise everyday things that can double up as flower vases – galvanized buckets, paint kettles, bottles, flower pots . . .

WHAT YOU NEED
A pair of good sharp secateurs or proper flower scissors is essential. You may need to cut wire sometimes, which ruins sharp blades, so you should invest

Left In late summer the large white blooms of mop-headed hydrangeas turn a cool pale green. Catch them fresh and fill a severe metal tureen with them, and when they have dried and turned crisp and papery, use them for winter decoration. Leaving hydrangea flower heads (on short stems) in a very small amount of water until it has all been drunk by the stems, is a foolproof way of drying them.

in a little pair of snips or wire cutters and keep them only for this job. Just occasionally you might need some damp florists' foam to put into the container in a block to hold the flower stems in place – it is particularly useful for big arrangements or for containers which don't hold water, but don't use it in clear glass where it would show. A dry version of this foam should be used with dried flowers to get a good dense overall texture from closely packed blooms. One old-fashioned way of holding stems steady is to crumple chicken wire in the neck of the vase to make a mesh to thread stems through; a more modern way is to sit heavy spiked stem holders at the bottom of the vase and spear on the flower stem ends to hold them securely. Both of these devices can give rather stiff results, so be careful how you use them.

One of the quickest and most effective ways to make an arrangement of flowers is to first make a posy or bunch in your hand, aiming for a rounded shape overall. Trim the stems to the same length and to fit into the container. Tie the whole thing together

loosely if you like, or simply slide the posy into a jug or vase and tweak it a bit until the flowers have settled down and look natural. It couldn't be easier, and always looks good with mixed varieties of flowers or bunches of all one type

Below The bright zingy colours of traditional Madras checked fabric take some living up to in terms of flowers. Mixed blue and red anemones can cope with the competition, having deep saturated colour which is further reinforced by the rich blue glass jug.

A Christmas Welcome

A Christmas garland hanging on the front door to welcome guests and decorate the house has become a tradition as appealing and well-loved as the tree indoors. The best garlands are generous and bold, and make use of natural materials wherever possible, particularly in a country setting where glittery decorations, plastic flowers, or satin bows somehow look at odds with the subdued winter garden surrounding the house. The base of the garland can be pine branches, holly, box or any suitable tough evergreen, then colour is added with fruits, nuts, dried flowers, spices, or whatever you like. The traditional colour scheme of red and green though seen a thousand times before never fails to please, but there is nothing to stop you using deep blues, oranges, or even shocking pink if you prefer.

If you would like to add some discreet sparkle then gild some of the nuts or fir cones with a dull gold paint, and choose ribbons with care if you are adding bows – natural fibres such as cotton velvets, torn fabrics, or antique silk all look much better than shiny man-made material.

This Christmas garland is made in the old-fashioned way on a wire frame padded with moss, which always gives a superb result and is well worth learning to make.

One Collect together all the materials you will need: a wire base, fine florist wire, stub wires, blue fir, and decorations such as nuts in their shells, dried cockscomb flowers, cranberries, small crab apples, pine cones, and ivy berries. Strong secateurs are essential and a glue gun is quick and easy for attaching nuts and berries to the fir.

Right The finished result looks rich and decorative, and though big, has been kept deliberately subtle and understated by not using ribbons or bright colours. Always make a garland a little too big rather than too small – this one, for instance, was made on a 45 cm (18 in) diameter wire frame, large enough to be well defined from a distance on the white porch.

Two Working flat on an old table or the floor, begin to pad the wire frame with handfuls of damp moss, wiring it round and round as you go. Work right round the frame until the whole thing is well covered and you have a good thick base to work onto. While the frame is still visible, it is a good idea to attach a wire loop for hanging the garland later.

Three Start to add short branches of the blue fir working round in one direction and overlapping each branch, wiring the cut end of the stem securely to the frame. Don't be afraid to use plenty of wire as it slides through the fir and doesn't show. You can always go round the frame again and add more to make the whole thing good and thick, but keep strictly to a round outline and try to keep the ring even.

Four Begin to add the nuts and fir cones to the branches; a glue gun makes this job speedy. Nestle the cones into the fir as if they were growing, and place the nuts and fruits at different angles. Cranberries or other soft things can be pushed onto short lengths of stub wire then lodged into the moss. Dried flowers and dried chillies can be wired if you want to re-use them, otherwise glue-gun into position.

A Wreath for all Seasons

A wreath or garland always has about it the feel of a celebration, of fun and festivity. A twisted vine base is the starting point to turn your inspiration into reality.

Top left SPRING The very fresh colour scheme of blue, green, and pale yellow is entirely in keeping with the first spring flowers. The material for this wreath has all been picked from a country garden, and includes small bunches of primroses, sprigs of forget-me-nots, pale green *helleborus corsicus*, a few of the first auriculas, and parrot green *euphorbia*.

Top right SUMMER The clear mauve flowers of clematis *Perle d'azure* mingle with two smaller flowered *viticella* clematis varieties in a darker purple and milky white colour. To provide contrast some variegated periwinkle foliage has been added throughout. It looks pleasing to see some of the vine tendrils and branches showing through among the flowers.

Bottom left AUTUMN There is much to choose from at this time of year but the warm russets and reds of berries and leaves always look good. It is sometimes easier to make bunches of plant material tied together with thin wire and then put into place, rather than threading individual small stems.

Bottom right WINTER This wreath is made by gluing the dried leaves, nuts, and fruits onto the vine garland. A glue gun is the best tool for this but you could use conventional glue although the construction time will be much longer while you wait for it to set. Ideal leaves are from *magnolia grandiflora* and *viburnum davidii* shrubs which turn a rich brown when dried. Other good materials are poppy seed-heads, dried pomegranates or mangosteens, and nuts in their shells: hazelnuts, pecans, walnuts, and brazils.

Above A hoop of twisted vine branches serves as the perfect base for floral and autumnal wreaths.

Making a wreath can be an elaborate and time consuming affair, or a spontaneous spur of the moment idea made real in no time at all. As a decoration for a birthday celebration, a wedding, or as an almost instant gift, it does not have to last for very long, and in this case, it can be made using a vine branch as the solid base onto which you thread and twine the stems of various flowers and leaves. Autumn and winter versions can be made, too, with dried materials that can be glued quickly into place.

The four versions here are all very different in feel and reflect the season in which they were made, but experiment and use flowers and materials of every kind to create your own special effects. Single colour wreaths look good, for instance, or try combining lots of hot clashing colours together; a single type of flower used generously can be pretty, too, as can a luxurious garland of full blown garden roses in a rainbow of pastel colours. Another ravishing version could be made from long strands of twining summer jasmine — it would not only look light and delicate with its starry flowers, but smell wonderful at the same time; yet another could be to use little bunches of winter berries, perhaps mixing green or black with red and orange ones, too.

Spring Bulbs for Winter Days

One of the greatest of joys during the bleakest months of the year are bowls of flowering bulbs to scent the house and bring colour and the hope of spring not far away.

To be sure of having indoor bulbs flowering when you want them to, first check that the bulbs you buy have been specially forced or prepared. Ordinary garden bulbs will flower even if planted indoors but it will be later, nearer to spring, and therefore not such a bonus.

It's possible to organize the timing of the flowering by holding some bulbs back a bit in colder conditions, and if you do that you can stagger the flowering to spread the pleasure a little longer. Most bought bulbs will come with instructions as to how long they

Top To plant in the conventional way in a bowl, you will need special bulb compost and marked labels to ensure recognition. Plant hyacinths quite close together but never touching, leaving the bulb tops just showing above the soil. Put into a dark cold cupboard, cellar or outhouse, or plunge under soil in the garden and leave for at least eight weeks.

Above When the shoots are at least 5 cm (2 in) tall, and there are signs of a good flower bud showing, the roots will have developed enough. At this stage the bowls can be moved into light, but not yet into warmth—an outside porch or cool bedroom are ideal. Once the shoots are green, cover the soil with moss if you like, then bring them into warmth and leave them to flower.

should be left to develop a good root system and sturdy shoots, but don't bring them into the light until the shoots (on hyacinths, for example) are at least 5 cm (2 in) high so that the bud is really well developed.

All kinds of bulbs can be grown in this way including tulips, narcissi, amaryllis, hyacinths, and crocuses. Hyacinths are one of the most rewarding to force, and you can grow them in all kinds of containers. Think beyond ordinary flower pots and use salad bowls, metal buckets, or any

container with enough depth to plant into; drainage holes are not necessary so you have a wide choice. The classic hyacinth glass has been popular since the seventeenth century and it is possible today to buy modern as well as Victorian or even Georgian ones in wonderful amethyst, amber, blue, and green glass. A single bulb sits in the top and sends roots down into the water below.

Top A collection of different hyacinth glasses being filled with water and a bulb; some people add a small piece of charcoal to the water to keep it sweet. The base of the bulb should only just touch the surface of the water so as not to waterlog the bulb. Either put the glasses away in a cold dark place or cover the tops with little paper cones.

Above The roots rapidly grow down into the water and make a pretty effect with light shining through them. Children enjoy watching this process, so give them a jar and a bulb of their own to grow. The shoots should be well developed before you remove the paper cover or bring the glass out into light. At first allow shoots to turn green then bring into warmth to force the flowers to open.

At certain times of year there is a wild bounty from the hedges, trees, and roadside. Steal a march on the birds and animals who soon find these riches, and bring home treats for yourselves, both edible and decorative.

Free from the Woods and Hedgerows

Gone are the days, thank goodness, of mass trips to the country by special train to plunder wild daffodils or snowdrops. We have laws now to prevent such vandalism, and a more caring attitude to our dwindling variety of plants and the animals who need them. But there are still some things which grow in profusion year after year and which survive any amount of collection of their fruit, seeds, or leaves and flowers. Always check before picking anything that it is not on a protected list.

Traditionally, there were regular harvests throughout the year to collect produce to make into wines or drinks, special preserves and healing potions – it was not so long ago that most medicines were herbal. So elderberry rob, for sore throats and colds, for instance, or raspberry leaf tea to help in childbirth. These and other items like jams and pickles were the kinds of things that were made to take up abundance when it occurred, and stored to be used when there was none.

A YEAR ROUND HARVEST
A favourite spring project for a child would be to fill a large shallow bowl with moss and into it tuck one or two of each small spring flower or special thing found on rambling walks. As well as being a lasting memento of a particular occasion, it would have special significance as a reminder of the start of the country year and everything coming to life again after winter.

A midsummer walk in country or suburb might produce a few heads of creamy elderflower which, when cooked with gooseberries or made into ice cream, impart a subtle muscat flavour which is mysterious and beguiling. Later in the year the flowers become deep purplish black berries which make a powerful-tasting sweet jelly or a delicious port-like wine.

Even during the winter months, there are always things to collect or find, such as skeleton seed-heads, or a few glossy berries that the birds have somehow missed, a hoard of empty striped snailshells, a few smooth perfect pebbles, or a lichen-covered twig.

Below left Autumn brings funghi and moss in the woods, and if you're lucky, nuts as well as edible berries. Funghi-hunting needs expert information and identification with a knowledgable guide, but other wild fruits and nuts are usually easy to check and identify. All this is irrelevant if you just want to use your gleanings as a decorative way to bring the changing seasons indoors. Fill bowls with sweet chestnuts and acorns; make simple wreaths with leaves and fluffy seed-heads; and display wild golden plums for a few days before submerging them in brandy or vodka to make a delicious liqueur.

Left Old-fashioned fruits, such as quince and medlar, are rarely found growing wild or cultivated these days but deserve to be revived as garden and hedgerow trees. The medlar has pale pink flowers in spring – very like quince flowers – but its fruits are small and brown, quite unlike the velvety and fragrant quinces.

Below In some seasons wild sweet chestnuts produce fruit large enough to eat in northern climates, but they are at their best in warmer conditions. Whatever size the floury nuts are, the wickedly spiny outer casings are decorative enough to use as simple arrangements.

Left Blackberries are the good part about brambles which are a menace once they have a thorny hold in the garden. The fruit is worth picking at every stage to decorate the house (you'll need thick gloves to do it, though), particularly when the berries are a mixture of green, red and ripe; and it is superlative made into that childhood favourite, bramble jelly, the perfect accompaniment for hot buttered toast.

A Handful of Herbs

Whether for cooking, curing or calming, herbs are always for aroma.

Although many old household and garden traditions have fallen by the wayside of progress and modern living, the custom of growing and using herbs has survived and is now even enjoying a period of great revival. There is certainly something rather magical about the scents and properties of many plants and of the processes that enable us to capture these aromas and use them long after the plant itself has withered. While we may no longer strew our floors with stems of rosemary and sweet rush, or stuff a mattress with lady's bed-straw, the use of sachets and sweet bags among stored clothes, or bunches of herbs hung to perfume a room and deter insects, is still perfectly practical. You don't need a specially planned herb garden to enjoy a herbal harvest; in fact many herbs—rosemary, thyme, savory, dwarf lavender, and parsley among them—are very happy growing in the confines of a pot or container.

In the kitchen the very best herbs are those freshly picked, and only a few are worth drying. Much more successful is to store herbs in a different way: by making them into pastes with oil such as the classic basil pesto, or infusing them in vinegar for special salad dressings, for instance. Or flavour old fashioned baked custards or rice puddings with a bay leaf or tiny sprig of rosemary.

Above Storecupboard treats to save for winter days or to give away as special gifts are easy to make and always pleasing. Tuck sprigs of fresh bay, thyme, and rosemary among small goat's cheeses placed in a sealed jar, cover with olive oil and flavour with garlic and seasoning. Infuse tarragon, dill, rosemary, basil, or savory in good wine vinegar and bottle. Make a clear apple jelly with extra lemon juice added, then flavour it with lavender, mint, or sweet geranium leaves; put into small pots and eat with savoury foods or as a spread on bread or toast.

Above Make simple flat fabric sachets and fill them with a herb mixture. Then place them between a pillowcase and pillow, or inside a much-loved cushion to give a gentle fragrance. The choice of herb is yours . . . hops to induce quiet sleep, lavender and rosemary to invigorate, or rose petals, jasmine or woodruff simply to smell divine.

Above The small decorative leaves of pelargoniums were immensely popular in Victorian and Edwardian times. At table, finger bowls were decorated with a single scented leaf and sweet dishes such as cakes and cold desserts perfumed from the huge range of aromas. Many varieties have lemon- or orange-scented leaves but there are eucalyptus, peach, absinthe, menthol, apple, peppermint, balsam, cedar, and rose fragrances, too. Find room on a windowsill for one at least, such as Rober's Lemon Rose.

Right Cut a small bunch of fresh rosemary, southernwood (a good anti-moth herb), sage, and *helichrysum plicatum*, and a few small bottles or plain stems of lavender. Tie the stems tightly together and hang from a ribbon on the back of a door, on a large piece of furniture, or from a chairback as here. The bouquet will dry slowly and quite naturally but retain lots of scent.

For as long as people have grown flowers, the rose has been a potent symbol as well as a useful herb for the still-room and kitchen, and a decorative flower in the house and garden. The thousands of varieties that we grow today have all been bred from the simple wild country rose.

Roses, Roses all the Way

Country roses are full and fat and very fragrant, with layers of petals and muddled centres in soft, dusky colours. They come in soft but strong subtle shades, from palest pearly white to deep, velvety purple, sometimes even striped and splashed in more than one colour. The bright clear colours of modern hybrid roses are often too strident to be sympathetic in the garden or house, though dried they provide rich material for winter bouquets and pot pourris. Even the smallest garden can find room for a shrub or two of roses and these can be grown happily in pots and containers if your patch is no more than a courtyard. If you have more space than this, then grow a mixture of perpetual flowering types to provide flowers throughout the summer as well as some of the old-fashioned roses which blossom in one dramatic flush in midsummer, filling the garden with scent and colour.

PETALS AND POTIONS
While one of the best and most simple of summer's pleasures must be a bowlful of roses newly picked from the garden, there are many ways of prolonging the pleasure by preserving the scents and hues of the petals. Original recipes for pot pourri are always based around rose petals as they retain their fragrance so well, and the soothing, healing properties of the rose have always been used in medicines and lotions. In the kitchen, rose petals can be used fresh to decorate cakes and pies and to flavour jams and ice creams; candied they will keep for months to adorn winter recipes. Choose varieties with a very strong fragrance and deep colour, usually red for pot pourris and lotions. Deep and pale pink petals are the prettiest for crystallizing and decorating food.

Below left Hang small bunches of garden roses to dry above a constant heat source. Pick the blooms when they have just opened out from the bud stage and they will open a little further as they dry. The colours stay fresh and bright and the process takes only a few days.

Below The finished roses can be collected throughout the summer months as they are cut, and dried. By the autumn you should have a generous display to use in winter decorations with other material, or you could simply leave them in a plain container which shows off their rich varied colours and textures as a reminder of balmy summer days.

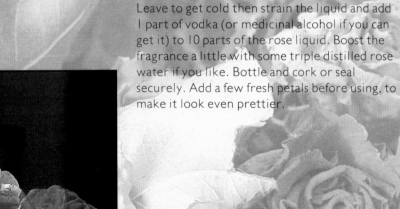

Above To make a simple rose skin lotion which is mild yet slightly astringent, infuse a jarful of fresh strongly scented petals in boiling water. Leave to get cold then strain the liquid and add 1 part of vodka (or medicinal alcohol if you can get it) to 10 parts of the rose liquid. Boost the fragrance a little with some triple distilled rose water if you like. Bottle and cork or seal securely. Add a few fresh petals before using, to make it look even prettier.

Left Store home-made lotions and flower waters in glass bottles and cork or seal well. Small flasks filled with the liquid make pretty presents, which are even better if the containers are old and unusual, such as antique perfume and medicine bottles.

Top There are several methods of crystallizing flower petals, but the best and easiest way is this. In a small screwtop jar dissolve 2 teaspoons of powdered gum arabic in enough distilled rose water to cover it. Shake occasionally and leave for about a day until you have a thick gummy solution. Paint dry rose petals with the gum, then dip in or sprinkle with fine sugar. Leave in a warm place on a wire rack until dry and crisp, then store in an airtight container. Use to decorate cakes and desserts.

Above The results look ravishing on a pile of palest pink meringues – and they are deliciously edible, too.

Sweet lavender must be the herb that everyone knows and loves best. With its fresh clean scent and deep mauve flower it never seems to go out of fashion.

Sweet Lavender, Fragrance of Forgotten Things . . .

The history of lavender as a household herb of great importance stretches back as far as we can find evidence of the way people lived. It has always been the 'laundry' herb *par excellence* and the name lavender is believed to come from the Latin verb *lavare*, meaning to wash. Wherever its name came from, lavender has always suggested and symbolized cleanliness and purity, and it has had all manner of healing uses: as a mild astringent for oily skins, as an antiseptic to help bruises heal quickly (it is a favourite herb in aroma-therapy), as a strewing herb and scent for soaps, polishes, and toilet waters, and as an anti-insect device.

There are dozens of varieties of both cultivated and wild lavender growing throughout the world, and although it appears to be primarily a sun-loving Mediterranean herb, certain types positively thrive in damper, more northern climates — and in fact produce some of the best lavender oils in these conditions. It flowers profusely and the fragrant oil it produces is easy to capture by distillation; at one time acres of land in southern France was carpeted in the dusky mauve blooms that provided the basic ingredient for lavender oil.

For the best scent or colour, choose your lavender variety with care. If you want deep colour and a good flower for drying, look for a dwarf variety such as 'Hidcote', while 'Grappenhall' and 'Old English' are larger plants that have a delicious, strong true lavender scent. Every garden should find room for some plants ideally grown somewhere near a path or gateway so that as you walk by you can squeeze a leaf or flower and release the clean, pungent aroma. If you have space to grow several varieties, then you can include some white- and pink-flowered versions as well as many of the more unusual wild species from the Mediterranean.

Above left The habit of putting dried lavender among stored clothes and laundry is a very old one. For shirts or blouses on hangers, make tiny wreaths by wiring dried lavender stems onto a wire circlet and looping them over the hook with a delicate ribbon.

Above To keep lavender flowers enclosed, make old-fashioned 'bottles'. Take 20 or so fresh long-stemmed flowers and make them into a bunch, tying securely just under the flower heads. Bend back each stem to enclose the flowers. Tie again below the flowers and put between layers of stored linen in airing cupboards and drawers.

Left Lavender is often used as a good inexpensive base for pot pourris. Here it is used alone and in great quantity to make a dramatic and very glamorous decoration. An antique foot bath has been filled with lavender off the stems and simply decorated with dried lemon peel.

Below Make lavender bath essence by infusing three handfuls of fresh lavender flowers in $\frac{1}{2}$ pint of vodka. Leave for 6 days, then strain. Add 5 drops of lavender essential oil, 2 tablespoons of both orange-flower water and rose water and about 4 tablespoons of distilled water. Shake thoroughly and keep in a narrow-necked bottle near the bath. Use sparingly.

Above A simple polish can be made by boiling a $\frac{1}{2}$ pint of water with a handful of lavender flowers. Leave to infuse for an hour, then strain. Reheat and add 2 ounces or about $\frac{1}{3}$ cup of shredded pure soap and leave until lukewarm. Melt 4 ounces or $\frac{1}{2}$ cup of beeswax in 1 pint of turpentine in a double saucepan (but not over direct heat), then add the soap mixture. Beat until creamy and add a few drops of lavender oil before pouring into small jars or pots. If you prefer, you can make equally fragrant polishes by substituting rosemary, or dried citrus peel.

Top Lavender has been the fragrance for home-made wood polishes since the days of strewing it fresh on earth floors and hanging it at windows to scent the room. This gentle polish is excellent for antique furniture and wood floors, and potted into small jars makes a good gift, too.

Accessorizing the Country Look **177**

Pot pourri came into the English language from the Spanish via the French and literally means a 'rotten pot'. The traditional method of making it involved a kind of fermentation using fresh flowers. It has the best fragrance of all pot pourris.

A Traditional Pot Pourri

Although powdered dried petals and spicy mixtures of herbs, roses, and fixatives had been used as household scents since medieval times, it was not until the mid-eighteenth century that the fragrant mixtures of flowers, spices, and oils now known as pot pourris were commonly made. It was then, too, that special jars to hold the delicious sweet mixtures (which were used to scent

One You will need a good supply of highly scented rose petals, preferably from old-fashioned roses – *Rosa gallica officinalis* is one of the best and has long been used in the perfume industry. Otherwise, any rose will do except a scentless florist's variety. Pick the petals off the stem and spread out to semi-dry in a warm place. On a hot summer day this will happen quite quickly outdoors. The petals should feel leathery when ready.

Two Next, make sure you have a good supply of sea or rock salt (not iodised). Now begin to layer up the semi-dry rose petals and coarse salt in a deep earthenware crock or large bowl. The proportions are about 10 cups of petals to 3 cups of salt. Put a plate or saucer on top of the petals then a heavy weight. Leave the bowl in a cool place and each day remove the plate and stir the mixture. Do this for about six weeks, until the petals have turned into a brown crumbly mixture.

Three Now you can have fun and add other scents and ingredients. Rose petals alone are fine but you can mix in dried scented flowers and leaves such as lavender, jasmine, crumbled bay leaves, rosemary, scented geraniums, lemon verbena, and so on, or dried citrus fruit peels and spices both whole or powdered such as cloves, nutmeg, cinnamon, tonka beans, vanilla pods, and allspice. Amounts will depend on how much mixture you have – add small spoonfuls first and keep mixing and smelling. Orris root powder is essential (it has been used for centuries as a fixative, to 'hold' scents), so allow 5 tablespoons for each 10 cups of rose petals. Finally, add a few drops of essential oil in whatever fragrance you like if the scent needs boosting.

rooms) first became popular. From the beginning, roses were a staple ingredient, and using this moist method a large amount of pot pourri could be made throughout the summer season.

Most of what we call pot pourri today is a mixture of dried flowers, leaves, and whatever looks pretty, impregnated with scented oils and fixatives; the materials themselves often have little scent of their own. If you have a source of fresh scented rose petals, try to make some of this traditional version instead.

Four This mixture should be stirred and tossed really thoroughly with a wooden spoon or your hands if you find this easier – the aim is to get the spices and the fixative throughout the petals and amalgamate everything well. The pot pourri should now be stored away for several more weeks to 'cure' and for the scents to mingle and fix. The best way to do this is to bag the mixture into paper – not plastic – bags and to clip the tops tightly shut (a clothes peg is ideal). Put the bags away in a cool dark place for six weeks, occasionally giving them a good shake.

Five The finished results of this pot pourri don't look particularly pretty, which is why it is usually covered up. Put the 'cured' pot pourri into lidded containers such as jars or baskets and cover. When you want to use it, stand the containers somewhere warm, remove the lids and enjoy the exquisite aroma.

Six Modern Pot Pourris

The quick and easy way to make pot pourri and scented flower mixtures is to use dried materials then add a fixative and fragrant essential oils. This means that the ingredients do not have to be scented in their own right, and you can play around with recipes to create textures and colour schemes way beyond the traditional.

Modern pot pourri recipes should still generally contain natural petals and leaves as a foundation to which other ingredients are added. Natural materials are best as obviously they have rich and subtle colours and take fragrances well. Some commercial pot pourris make use of all kinds of dubious dyed ingredients, such as wood shavings, which may work well at absorbing oils but do not provide enough visual interest. Look out for well-shaped seed pots and small dried fruits, berries, and stems; and all kinds of whole spices and dried fruit peels. Many different types of dried leaf are pretty, too, and so are mosses and lichens.

The best effects are obtained from keeping to a simple but strong colour theme and considering the container which will hold the finished result. Once you have collected together all the dried materials, put them into a large bowl and add ground and whole spices if you are using them. You can do without a fixative if you are happy to replenish with essential oils quite often, otherwise use powdered orris root at about 2 tablespoons to every 10 cups of dried petals, etc. Mix this well into the ingredients, then add a few drops of essential oil of your choice and keep stirring. Sniff and assess and keep adding oil. When you are happy with the look and smell, transfer the mixture to paper bags, close the tops, and put away 'to cure' for six weeks in a dark, dry place before using.

All the pot pourris here were made by this method, and in each case a colour theme was chosen which decided the ingredients to use.

Blue bowl (top, left) Dried orange peel, lavender, larkspur, French marigolds, pot marigolds, cinnamon, whole cloves, rose hips, rose petals. Oils—lavender and orange.

Orange bowl (above, left) Beech mast, dried orange peel, rosemary, bay leaves, hydrangea, dried lime peel, iris berries. Oils—rosemary and lime.

Mauve bowl (top, centre) Lavender, hibiscus, mallow, purple tulip, mahonia berries. Oil—violet or lavender.

Pink bowl (above, centre) Eucalyptus leaves, pink rose petals, pink tulips. Oil—tea rose.

Red bowl (top, right) Deep red roses, hibiscus, pomanders, red chillies, whole nutmegs, rose hips, cinnamon bark, cockscomb, peonies, cloves. Oils—pine, juniper, neroli.

Turquoise bowl (above, right) Yellow tulips, daffodils, freesia, ranunculus, marigold, coreopsis, cedar wood chippings, dried lemon peel. Oils—jasmine, cedarwood, bergamot.

A table in any room becomes a focus of attention whether it is being used for a meal or not. Flowers, fruits, vegetables, and all kinds of containers can be combined to make centrepieces.

Clever Centrepieces

Although it might appear that anything goes when it comes to decorating a table, just remember that if a meal is planned then it is the food which is most important. Avoid enormous and elaborate arrangements or flowers which are overpoweringly scented. Everyday family meals need not miss out even if all you have time for is to make a pretty dish of fruits or fresh vegetables, perhaps part of the meal or perhaps not, to stand in the centre of the table. On grander occasions, when the crisp linen comes out and cutlery is bright and sparkling, you should choose slightly more sophisticated flowers even if they are home-grown or collected. If you don't own much in the way of suitable vases or containers then pull anything into action, raiding the kitchen for suitable things such as baking tins, low baskets or glass tumblers. You can always build an arrangement straight into foam and stand this on a waterproof base, or if you particularly want a low spreading arrangement to fill up a large area of the table.

Top This must be one of the quickest ideas to put together. The ingredients are chunky fir cones but you could choose fruit. They are piled into an old fashioned *comportère* and decorated with an antique silk-satin ribbon tied with a flourish through one of the handles.

Above A small garden trug basket makes a perfect container for a collection of yellow and orange fruits with scented *narcissi*. For a mealtime flowers can be cut and put into the arrangement, then put into water later.

Top A simple unadorned wooden table set for an informal meal needs decorating in suitable harmony. The Mexican metal platter is the starting point for a group of burgundy red pears and glowing red peppers set off by a hot scarlet chilli.

Above Little collections of seeds, fruits, and berries have been used to fill the sections of an old spice box to make a tablescape which is infinitely variable. Any small containers would work equally well for this idea.

Far left A dinner party deserves a special centrepiece such as this low one built into foam. It is a spring mixture of hyacinths, white tulips and scented flowering shrubs from the garden. Shop-bought flowers are always improved by a few pieces of natural foliage mixed in.

Winter time in the country demands warm, cheerful colours and inviting candlelight. All kinds of special decorations can be made from fruits and berries to celebrate winter festivals and holidays from Thanksgiving to Christmas.

Festive Centrepieces

When candlelight was the only way to see in the dark, there was probably little romance or magic in the warm flickering wax flames. Now that we have other options, however, we use candles as a special effect to create an atmosphere, to turn a gathering of people into a party, or to enliven decorations. Candles enthrall us in the way that a living, crackling open fire does, and they have become an almost essential part of most winter festivities.

The simplest candle ideas are invariably the best, from night lights dropped into glass jars ranged along a window frame to a collection of fat creamy beeswax candles grouped on a reflective surface. Cream or white ones have more elegance and charm than any coloured versions and are invariably cheaper, too. Be sure to have a stock of small plain white candles, nightlights, and little Christmas-tree-sized candles as well as the tiny tapers which can be used to decorate desserts, special cakes, or flower decorations.

Natural materials make elegant centrepieces too, and even when the colours of summer have long faded there are still bright jewels to be found in trees and hedgerows. Clusters of glossy berries often remain on bare stems until they are eaten by the birds, and they make the perfect basis for simple autumnal festive centrepieces and decorations. If you can't do your own harvesting then use seasonal fruits from the shops.

Top A pair of old metal cheese drainers have found a new life as simple but very effective candle holders. Once lit they cast pinpricks of light, and make a warm glow to cheer a dark corner of any room. Metal moulds of all kinds are suitable as candle containers, and when they are new add extra reflections and sparkle.

Above Several different types of berries and rose hips have been made into small bunches in this centrepiece. They include mistletoe, ivy berries, pyracantha berries, rose hips, and cotoneaster berries. Each bunch was tied tightly round the stems and wrapped in small white paper doilies, then packed tightly into a basket. Finally, thin white taper candles were pushed in among the bunches. These candles burn quite quickly so should never be left alight without someone watching over them.

Top This combination of glossy red apples and nightlights, is one of the most spectacular candle ideas to make. Slice off a small section across the top of each apple and hollow out a space for a nightlight to sit inside without showing above the top edge. For the best effect make a long row of these apples on a shelf or window sill, or on a mantel as here.

Above Clementines or tangerines make wonderful candle holders for small white candles. You can usually push the candles into the skin easily enough but use a sharp knife to break the skin first if you can't.

Right A fine old Wedgewood plate was the inspiration for an easy decoration made by filling metal biscuit cutters with cranberries and popped corn.

Right These little boxes are made from many different woods and designed for many purposes, from holding calling cards or spices to tea and collar studs. Brought together and stood on a desk, they glow harmoniously.

Right A collection of collections in a country cupboard. Toy trucks and buses mingle with oilcans, maps with ink bottles. Several different book collections are on the go as well, and everything merges into a delightfully busy and interesting mix.

Country Collections

The relaxed and easy country look usually contains collections of all kinds. These might be family treasures or quirky 'finds', rewards from a lifetime of auction sales or simply things which seem to have multiplied without anyone really noticing.

Below Collecting singles of something which was once sold as sets is an inexpensive hobby. A cup and saucer bought occasionally soon builds into a large collection. Here the theme is mostly floral but anything pretty and delicate seems to fit.

Most of us have a collecting habit even if we aren't really conscious of it. Some people like to have rows of jars and good things on pantry shelves, or chests filled with linen or towels. Many of us keep photos, or childrens' first drawings, memorabilia and souvenirs from trips abroad, or shells from a beach, without even thinking of them as a collection – the most everyday and ordinary objects brought together can be decorative and interesting.

A big earthenware bowl for example would make the perfect home for a collection of shards and found pieces of broken china, while a bright papier mâché dish would be suitable for a collection of shells and small pebbles.

Larger collections or groups of bigger things need to be planned more carefully if they fill a tabletop, desk, or bookshelves and therefore take valuable space from a room, but many country collections are useful in themselves and are not seen exclusively as a decoration; things such as antique woodworking tools, baskets old and new, pitchers and jugs, terracotta pots, or hats.

Left A pretty wavy-edged cane table makes a perfect background for a collection of sea shells. The arrangement is carefully laid out, making use of larger shells to hold miniature collections of their own. The witty candle shade completes the whole picture.

Left A collection of antique blown eggs, displayed simply on sand in an oval fluted dish. It is illegal to collect birds' eggs nowadays, but old collections still exist and are passed down through families.

Casual Collections

Collections can happen without much effort; you can come across things discarded by nature or man, or you might inherit someone else's passionate finds. They need not be valuable, and nature usually provides the most decorative things of all.

Below Ragged and ancient nests put together in a detailed Victorian basket make a miniature landscape of texture and colour, combined with twigs and oakmoss lichen. Modern-day birds still use cobwebs, hair, and moss for their nests, and occasionally add plastic string, too.

Some of the prettiest collections are of natural things discarded or ignored by most people; before collecting anything from the wild, though, you must be cautious. Only remove things which are truly finished with. Certain things cannot be collected legally these days; for example, birds' nests should only be removed at least a season after their use when there is no possibility that they may be used again.

Sea shells from exotic coasts can be bought, but do check that they have not been harvested live and are genuinely discarded and empty. Safer territory are sea-washed pebbles of all types which are fun to find on most beaches, as well as dried seaweeds, driftwood, pieces of multi-coloured fishing net, and other maritime detritus. Seeds and nuts of all kinds are often so abundant that they can be collected, too, but sow a few to grow into plants as your personal campaign to give nature a helping hand.

Displays on the Level

In most houses horizontal surfaces can easily get filled with clutter. Organize good storage first for everything which is best kept out of sight, then you have room to make the most of the things you want to have on view.

A few purists insist on living in simple empty spaces with the minimum of stuff around them. Bare walls, things kept behind cupboard doors, and clean bare surfaces everywhere suit a certain lifestyle, but they rarely fit with the country way of doing things. Country rooms come to their current state by a long process of accumulation and development, and often much of what is in them is there for purely practical purposes. Things need to be on hand and there isn't always room for everything to be stored away; besides, good furniture for this purpose has always been expensive, so improvisation has usually been the answer in all but the grandest houses. Out of this tradition has come the idea of surfaces as a place to put things purely for decoration – the wide mantel shelf holding candles, the all-important clock, a pair of treasured china plates or figures arranged into a pleasing and often symmetrical arrangement, for instance.

Table surfaces are often more informal, with a mixture of useful and decorative things mixed in a haphazard but appealing way. A lamp to cast a pool of light or to read by, some fresh flowers, perhaps, or a bowl of pot pourri, and a stack of tempting books. Space should always be left on surfaces near seating for the odd cup of coffee, pair of spectacles or halfread

newspaper, as nothing is worse than a total covering of every horizontal surface with small scale clutter.

Hall tables are a good place to make a welcoming and decorative display in a space which is usually only passed through, but once again there should be some space to park a bunch of keys or

the morning post. Kitchen surfaces are more contentious as some cooks insist on clear workspace before they can be creative. And a country kitchen just isn't the heart of the house without a bit of clutter, whether it's a bowl of fruit or vegetables fresh from the garden, or bunches of herbs.

Left A round tabletop has been draped in a richly complicated floral patterned fabric; from this cue come the decorations of an old painted basket filled with auricula plants echoing the fabric flowers, and a small collection of treen.

Above When flowers are abundant why restrict the pleasure they give? A mix of materials here includes wooden decoy ducks, old pewter, modern metal candlesticks, and ancient cream china which holds a mass of spring flowers.

*We tend to be hidebound when
it comes to what we hang on
walls. Of course they are the
place for mirrors and pictures,
but they can also be the
backdrop to an awful lot more
besides.*

Wall Displays

Country walls can be lumpy and bumpy,
but in rooms which are often small and
lacking space to put things away, they
become obvious places to store and
display all manner of objects.

The country style of picture is likely
to be inherited, perhaps a portrait, or a
drawing of a child or animal. There
isn't usually room for great art but
rather a desire to be surrounded by
homely pictures that have become old
friends. Landscapes and country
subjects have always been popular, even
though the real thing is probably just
outside the doorstep.

A mirror is important for
straightening a hat or hair, and often to
maximize on the little light which falls
into small-windowed rooms.
Mementoes play a part, too, and hooks
are useful to hold bunches of keys, a
clutch of cards, a calendar or string.
Practical objects can often look
decorative with just a little care spent
on what you use to hang them up with.

A patchwork of shapes and textures covers an
old beamed wall. A variety of pleasures are
reflected in the eclectic mix of paintings,
lighting, garlands, and mementoes which
manage to look good together in a
complementary way.

Above Built-in narrow shelves are arranged above a wide open span of cupboards on the dresser principle. Painted in a soft matt blue-green, the shelves hold not just books but pictures, cards, objects, and clouds of genista in a large scale vase.

Left A very unusual Welsh shelved corner cupboard makes a dramatic decorative focus to a room when it is filled with odd treasures and simple flowers in bright glowing colours.

The shelf was probably the first and best arrangement ever made to store things. You can have a shelf of some kind to keep most things you are ever likely to want kept. Simple planks on brackets or rows within fine furniture, every house needs them.

Shelves that Work

There are few drawbacks to shelves as storage except possibly keeping things clean if they aren't used often. Of course this problem led to the evolution of cupboards – which were originally shelves with doors, and then later glazed doors in front of shelves.

One of the nicest and cheapest ways of making a kitchen work is still to create simple rows of shelves to hold all the paraphernalia that you might need. You can make this idea a little more sophisticated by using boxes, baskets or other graded containers to stand on the shelves and keep different things separate inside them. Shelves can be rough unpainted timber or fine oak, slate, stone, marble, painted wood, wire, metal or delicate slats, the choice is wide and is often made according to the walls on which they are going to be fixed.

If plain shelves are not for you, then the choice of furniture incorporating shelves is enormous. Sometimes a compromise is the best solution for crooked country walls, having shelves and cupboards built in as permanent furniture rather like an old fashioned kitchen dresser. This allows wobbly plastering and bent door frames to be assimilated into the overall plan rather than trying to get off-the-peg storage to fit.

Never underestimate the need for storage, and particularly shelves. They do not have to stretch across a complete wall to be useful: short shelves in a bank from floor to ceiling are good to have for things such as recipe books in a kitchen or small bottles and jars in a bathroom. The arrangement looks neat, too, keeping everything in a small solid block, and makes use of narrow areas of wall between doors and windows, for example.

Below A classic pine kitchen dresser, still functional but with decorative overtones, in a country dining room. A patchwork mix of lovingly collected blue and white china fills the shelves and overflows onto the surface below.

Self Contained

Every room that is used for a practical purpose needs storage of a systematic and organized kind. A kitchen, for example, needs a filing system in just the same way that an office does. The country ways of doing this are ingenious, being thrifty, sensible and good looking, too.

Below A healthy taste for olive oil can mean unlimited storage for small and awkward kitchen tools, and other odd items.

Shelves are great as a basic means of storage but there does come a time when something slightly more sophisticated is necessary to keep things apart. This can take the form of rows of baskets, boxes, glass jars or even old tins. The trick in making this idea work visually is to coordinate the containers in some way. Either choose things that are all exactly alike, or are made alike by you with a coat of paint or whatever is necessary. Or keep them the same by using only things made from one material (such as wood) even if they are all different sizes, or go for a jazzy mix of colours united by the original purpose of the container. For kitchen foods you generally need storage which has a lid to keep things clean, and basic glass jars with stoppers are still the best-looking option. If your containers are not transparent, remember you will need some obvious but discreet labelling.

Left A shelf system has been built in this garden shed to hold precious old terracotta pots safely on their sides. They look neat and decorative, too. The wooden box at the bottom holds broken crocks for pot drainage.

Left A slatted wooden rack above a work bench is designed to store small garden tools. The flat area beneath is perfect for filling pots with soil and sowing seeds, which are stored in a solid wooden mouseproof box nearby.

Outdoor Organization

From out of doing or making things comes an understanding of how to organize space, tools, and time. A garden shed or outdoor workshop needs exactly the same treatment.

Below Wooden-chip boxes first used as crates for new potatoes are recycled into storage for odds and ends, such as plant labels, raffia, seeds, and gardening gloves.

Outdoor storage is really no different to organization indoors. Inevitably things must be strong and sturdy, but materials can be rougher, finishes less perfect than their equivalent inside a house. Walls play an important part again, as here they are not needed for purely decorative purposes so can be pressed into really useful service — long-handled garden tools are dangerous left leaning just waiting to be tripped over, but they can be filed away in rows hanging from hooks or slats.

Gardening stuff quickly gets messy and needs strict containment to avoid leaking seed packets and tangled garden twine. Hang up as much stuff as possible and find a few sensible containers for delicate things, such as seeds and bulbs. Big plastic or metal bins make good storage for composts and fertilizers, and old baskets can become home to gardening gloves or favourite small tools such as secateurs. Flower pots and seed trays have a habit of building themselves into wobbling turrets before you realize it, so sort them into similar sizes and stack them on their sides.

Laura Ashley Shops Around the World

UNITED KINGDOM

LONDON SHOPS
BRENT CROSS Brent Cross Shopping Centre, NW4
(clothes only) 081 202 2679
CHELSEA 120 Kings Road, SW3 4TR 071 823 7550
COVENT GARDEN 35/36 Bow Street, WC2E 7AU
071 240 1997
EALING 5 The Broadway, W5 2NH 081 579 5197
KENSINGTON 96b Kensington High Street, W8
071 938 3751
KNIGHTSBRIDGE 47/49 Brompton Road, SW3 1DE
(clothes only) 071 823 9700
KNIGHTSBRIDGE 7/9 Harriet Street, SW1 (home
furnishings only) 071 235 9797
MARBLE ARCH 449/451 Oxford Street, W1 071 355 1363
OXFORD CIRCUS 256/258 Regent Street, W1R 5DA
071 437 9760

COUNTRY SHOPS
ABERDEEN 44/45 Bon Accord Centre, George Street,
AB1 1BP 0224 625787
AYLESBURY 10 Hale Leys, Buckinghamshire IP20 1ST
0296 84574
BANBURY 43 Market Place, Oxfordshire OX16 8NW
0295 271295
BARNET 22 The Spires, Hertfordshire EN5 5UZ
081 449 9866
BATH The Old Red House, 8/9 New Bond Street, Avon
BA1 1BE 0225 460341
BEDFORD 75 High Street, Bedfordshire MK40 1NE
0234 211416
BELFAST 53-54 Castle Court Centre, Royal Avenue,
BT1 1DD 0232 233313
BEVERLEY 36/40 Toll Gavel, Humberside HU17 9AR
0482 872444
BIRMINGHAM 28 The Pavilions Shopping Centre, 38 High
Street, West Midlands B4 7SE 021 631 2842
BISHOPS STORTFORD 17 South Street, Hertfordshire
CM23 3AB 0279 655613
BOLTON 2 Victoria Plaza, Oxford Street, Lancashire
BL1 1RD 0204 363017
BOURNEMOUTH 58 Commercial Road, Dorset BH2 1LR
(clothes only) 0202 5239764
BOURNEMOUTH 80 Old Christchurch Road, Dorset
BH1 1LR (home furnishings only) 0202 557572
BRIGHTON 45 East Street, Sussex BN1 1HN 0273 205304
BRISTOL 62 Queen's Road, Clifton, Avon BS8 1RE
0272 277468
BRISTOL The Galleries, Broadmead, Avon BS1
0272 221011
BROMLEY 62 High Street, Kent BR1 1EY 081 290 6620
BURY ST. EDMUNDS 1 The Lexicon, Cornhill, Suffolk
IP33 1BT 0284 755658
CAMBRIDGE 14 Trinity Street, Cambridgeshire CB2 1TB
0223 351378
CANTERBURY 41/42 Burgate, Kent CT1 2HB 0227 450961
CARDIFF 6 Queens West Precinct, Queen Street, South
Glamorgan CF1 4AH 0222 340808
CARLISLE 3/4 Grapes Lane, The Lanes, Cumbria CA3 8NH
0228 48810
CHELMSFORD 10/13 Grays Brewery Yard, Springfield
Road, Essex CM2 6QR 0245 359602
CHELTENHAM 100 The Promenade, Gloucestershire
GL50 1NB 0242 580770
CHESTER 50 Eastgate Row, Cheshire CH1 1LF (clothes
only) 0244 313964
CHESTER 17/19 Watergate Row, Watergate Street,
Cheshire CH1 2LE (home furnishings only) 0244 316403
CHICHESTER 32 North Street, West Sussex PO19 1LX
0243 775255
COLCHESTER 4/5 Trinity Square, Essex CO1 1JR
0206 562692
CROYDON 11/12 Drummond Place, North End, Surrey
CR0 1TQ 081 688 5177
DERBY 8 Albert Street, Derbyshire DE1 2DS 0332 361642
DUDLEY 89 Merry Hill Centre, Brierley Hill, West
Midlands DY5 1SY 0384 79730

EASTBOURNE 129/131 Terminus Road, East Sussex
BN21 3NR 0323 411955
EDINBURGH 126 Princes Street, Midlothian EH2 4AH
(clothes only) 031 225 1218
EDINBURGH 90 George Street, Midlothian EH2 4JY (home
furnishings only) 031 225 1121
EXETER 41/42 High Street, Devon EX4 3AJ 0392 53949
FARNHAM The Barn, Lion & Lamb Yard, Surrey GU9 7LL
0252 712812
GATESHEAD 7 The Parade, Metro Centre, Tyne & Wear
NE11 9YJ 091 493 2411
GLASGOW 84/90 Buchanan Street, Strathclyde G1 3HA
041 226 5040
GUILDFORD 71/72 North Street, Surrey 0483 34152
HARROGATE 3 James Street, North Yorkshire HG1 1QS
0423 526799
HEREFORD 7 Commercial Street, Herefordshire HR1 2DB
0432 272446
HIGH WYCOMBE 30 White Hart Street, Buckinghamshire
HP11 2HL 0494 442394
HITCHIN 121/123 Bancroft, Hertfordshire SG5 1LS
0462 420445
HORSHAM 3/4 Middle Street, West Sussex RH12 1NW
0403 59052
IPSWICH 17 The Buttermarket, Suffolk IP1 1BQ
0473 216828
KING'S LYNN 48/49 High Street, Norfolk PE33 1BE
0553 768881
KINGSTON 32/33 Market Place, Surrey KT1 1JH
081 549 0055
LEAMINGTON SPA 108 The Parade, Warwickshire
CV32 4AQ 0926 314584
LEEDS Church Institute, 9 Lands Lane, West Yorkshire
LS1 6AW 0532 4506222
LEICESTER 6 Eastgate, Leicestershire LE1 4FB 0533 513165
LINCOLN 310 High Street, Lincolnshire LN5 7DR
0522 511611
LIVERPOOL 16 Clayton Square, Merseyside L1 1HN
051 709 5556
LLANIDLOES 30 Great Oak Street, Powys SY18 6BW
05512 2557
MAIDSTONE 8/10 King Street, Kent ME14 1DE
0622 750138
MANCHESTER 28 King Street, Greater Manchester
M2 6AY 061 834 7335
MIDDLESBROUGH 48 Linthorpe Road, Cleveland
TS1 1RA 0642 226034
MILTON KEYNES 40/42 Midsummer Arcade,
Buckinghamshire MK9 3BB 0908 660190
NEWCASTLE-UNDER-LYME 45/57 High Street,
Staffordshire ST5 1PN 0782 662014
NEWPORT 36 High Street, Isle of Wight PO33 2HT
0983 821806
NORTHAMPTON 3b Peacock Place, Northamptonshire
NN1 2DP (clothes only) 0604 231975
NORWICH 19 London Street, Norfolk NR2 1JE
0603 632958
NOTTINGHAM 1, 6 Clumber Street, Nottinghamshire
NG1 3GA 0602 503366
OXFORD 26/27 Cornmarket Street, Oxfordshire
OX1 3BY 0865 791689
PERTH 189/191 High Street, Perthshire PH1 5UN
0738 23141
PETERBOROUGH 90 Queensgate Centre, Cambridgeshire
PE1 1NS 0733 311766
PLYMOUTH 5 The Armada Centre, Mayflower Street,
Devon PL1 1LE 0752 268344
PRESTON 32 Fishergate, Lancashire PR1 2ED 0772 202425
READING 75/76 Broad Street, Berkshire RG1 2AP
0734 594313
RICHMOND 44/45 George Street, Surrey TW9 1HJ
081 940 9556
ST ALBANS 13 Market Place, Hertfordshire AL3 5DR
0727 864611
ST HELIER 1/3 Beresford Street, Jersey 0534 20252
ST PETERS PORT Rara Limited, 4 Mansell Street,
Guernsey 0481 28222

SALISBURY 7 New Canal, Wiltshire SP1 2AA 0722 338383
SCARBOROUGH 25 Brunswick Pavilion, North Yorkshire
YO11 1VE 0723 377537
SHEFFIELD, 56 Park Lane, Meadowhall Centre, South
Yorkshire S9 1EL 0742 568221
SHEFFIELD 87 Pinstone Street, South Yorkshire S1 2HJ
0742 701855
SHREWSBURY 2 Charles Darwin Centre, Pride Hill,
Shropshire SY1 1OX 0743 351467
SKIPTON 13 Craven Court, North Yorkshire BD23 1DS
0756 700301
SOLIHULL 124, High Street, West Midlands B91 3SX
021 704 4344
SOUTHAMPTON 2 Above Bar Church, Hampshire
SO1 0FE 0703 228944
SOUTHEND-ON-SEA 107 High Street, Essex SS1 1LQ
0702 333090
SOUTHPORT 465/467 Lord Street, Merseyside PR9 0AQ
0704 546214
STOCKPORT 2 Warren Street, Cheshire SK1 1UD
061 474 7927
STRATFORD-UPON-AVON 41/42 Henley Street,
Warwickshire CV37 6QV 0789 298852
SUTTON 3/4 Times, 2 High Street, Surrey SM1 1LF
081 643 9790
SUTTON COLDFIELD 164 The Parade, Gracechurch
Centre, West Midlands B72 1PH 021 355 3671
SWINDON 19e Regent Street, Wiltshire SN1 1JL
0793 641727
TAUNTON 2/4 High Street, Somerset TA1 3PG
0823 288202
TENTERDEN 19/21 High Street, Kent TN30 6BN
0580 65188
TORQUAY 74 Fleet Street, TQ2 5EB 0803 291443
TRURO 2, 7 Pydar Street, Cornwall TR1 2AR 0872 223019
TUNBRIDGE WELLS 61 Calverley Road, Kent TN1 2UY
0892 534431
WATFORD 1 The Parade, High Street, Hertfordshire
WD1 1LQ 0923 54411
WILMSLOW 17 Grove Street, Cheshire, SK9 5EG
0625 535331
WINCHESTER 126 High Street, Hampshire SO23 9AX
0962 855716
WINDSOR 32 Peascod Street, Berkshire SL4 1EA (clothes
only) 0753 854345
WINDSOR 99/101 Peascod Street, Berkshire SL4 1DH
(home furnishings only) 0753 831456
WOLVERHAMPTON 54/55 Dudley Street, West Midlands
WV1 3ER 0902 27293
WORCESTER Crown Passage, Broad Street,
Worcestershire WR1 3LL 0905 20177
WORTHING 1/2 Montague Centre, West Sussex
BN11 1YU 0903 205160
YEOVIL 28 Vicarage Walk, Quedam Centre, Somerset
BA20 1EX 0935 79863
YORK 7 Davygate, North Yorkshire YO1 2QR
0904 627707

REPUBLIC OF IRELAND SHOPS
DUBLIN 60/61 Grafton Street, Dublin 2 01 679 5433
CORK 9/10 Merchants Quay Shopping Centre, Patrick
Street 021 274070

OTHER SHOPS
NEWPORT 36 High Street, Isle of Wight PO33 2HT
0983 821806
ST HELIER 1/3 Beresford Street, Jersey 0534 20252
ST PETERS PORT Rara Limited, 4 Mansell Street,
Guernsey 0481 28222

HOMEBASES
Within Sainsbury's Homebase House and Garden Centres
BASILDON Old London Road, Vange, Essex SS16 4PR
0268 584088
BASINGSTOKE Winchester Road, Hampshire RG22 6HN
0256 469510
BATH Pines Way, Avon BA2 3ET 0225 339293
BLACKHEATH 241 Kidbrooke Park Road, London SE3 9PP

081 856 9767
BRADFORD 762 Harrogate Road, Greengate, West
Yorkshire BD10 0QF 0274 611929
BRANKSOME Redlands, Parkstone, Poole, Dorset
BH12 1DN 0202 768311
BRENTFORD Syon Lane, Isleworth, Middlesex TW7 5NP
081 847 2214
CAMBERLEY 560 London Road, Surrey GU15 3XS
0276 686227
CARDIFF Colchester Avenue, Roath, South Glamorgan
CF3 7AN 0222 499675
CATFORD 10 Beckenham Hill Road, London SE6
081 461 0606
CHELMSFORD Riverside Park, Victoria Rd, Essex
CM1 1PG 0245 257257
CHICHESTER 4 Portfield Retail Park, West Sussex
PO19 4HN 0243 533373
COLCHESTER St Andrews Avenue, Essex CO4 3BG
0206 869187
COVENTRY Junction Fletchampstead Highway Sir Henry
Parkes Road, Canley, West Midlands CV5 6RG 0203 715901
CRAWLEY Crawley Avenue, West Green, Surrey
RH10 2NF 0293 538351
CRAYFORD Stadium Way, Near Dartford, Kent DA1 4HN
0322 558614
CROYDON 66a Purley Way, Surrey CR0 3LP 081 684 8250
DERBY Kingsway, Derbyshire DE3 3NF 0332 291260
GLOUCESTER St Oswalds Road, Gloucestershire GL1 2UI
0452 526806
GUILDFORD Ladymead Retail Park, Ladymead, Surrey
0483 304115
HARLOW 3 Queensgate Centre, Edinburgh Way, Essex
CM20 2SU 0279 413355
HATFIELD Oldings Corner, Comet Way, Hertfordshire
AL9 5JP 0707 275837
HENDON Rookery Way, The Hyde, London NW9 6SS
081 200 7737
HULL Priory Sidings, Sainsbury Way, Hessle Road,
Humberside HU13 9NT 0482 572434
ILFORD 714/720 High Road, Seven Kings, Essex IT3 5RS
081 590 0212
IPSWICH Felixstowe Road, Suffolk IP3 8TQ 0473 721124
KENSINGTON 193/195 Warwick Road, London W14 8PU
071 603 2285
KINGSTON 229/253 Kingston Road, New Malden, Surrey
KT3 3RU 081 949 7861
LEEDS Moor Allerton Centre, King Lane, West Yorkshire
LS17 5NY 0532 685010
LEICESTER 37 Putney Road, off Welford Road,
Leicestershire LE2 7TF 0533 546075
LUTON Enterprise Way, Bedfordshire LU3 4BW
0582 593445
MAIDSTONE Aylesford Retail Park, London Road, Kent
ME20 7TP 0622 715400
MIDDLETON Heaton Park Road West, Higher Blackley,
Manchester M9 3QS 061 740 5700
MILL HILL Pentavia Retail Park, Watford Way, NW7
081 203 7740
MILTON KEYNES 800 Grafton Gate West, Central Milton
Keynes, Buckinghamshire MK9 1DJ 0908 69272
NEWCASTE-UNDER-LYME 33 Brook Lane, Staffordshire
ST5 3HU 0782 711752
NEW SOUTHGATE 3 Station Road, London N11 1QJ
081 368 1698
NORTHAMPTON Victoria Promenade, Northamptonshire
NN1 1HH 0604 234143
NORWICH Roundtree Way, Mousehold Lane, Norfolk
NR7 8SH 0603 417474
NOTTINGHAM Castle Marina Park, Castle Boulevard,
Nottinghamshire NG7 1GY 0602 413885
OLDBURY 50 Halesowen Street, Warley, West Midlands
B69 2AN 021 544 7333
ORPINGTON Seven Oaks Way, BR5 3HQ 0689 890353
OXFORD Horspath Driftway, Headington OX3 7NJ
0865 747919
PENGE 45 Oakfield Road, Off Penge High Street, London
SE20 8RB 081 778 4214
RAYLEIGH WEIR 23 Stadium Way, Benfleet, Essex
SS7 3UB 0268 745374
READING 50 Kenavon Drive, Berkshire RG1 3DH
0734 584572
ROCHESTER Horstead Retail Park, Maidstone Road,
Chatham, Kent HE5 9ME 0634 200088

ROMFORD Rom Valley Way, Essex RM7 0AJ 0708 730326
SHEFFIELD 401 Chesterfield Road, Woodseats, South
Yorkshire S8 0RW 0742 555175
SOUTHAMPTON Lordshill Shopping Centre, Hampshire
SO1 8HH 0703 739763
STOCKPORT 4 Great Portwood Street, Cheshire
SK1 2HH 061 474 7489
SWANSEA Quay Parade, West Glamorgan SA1 8JP
0792 650935
SWINDON Paddington Drive, Churchward, Wiltshire
SN5 7YN 0793 487125
WAKEFIELD Ing's Road, West Yorkshire WF1 1RS
0924 387011
WALSALL 1 Bradford Place, West Midlands WS1 1PL
0922 29524
WALSGRAVE 459 Ansty Road, Coventry CV2 3BQ
0203 602086
WALTHAM CROSS Sturlas Way, Hertfordshire EN8 7BE
0992 25275
WALTHAMSTOW 2c Fulbourne Road, London E17
081 531 8233
WATFORD 114 St. Albans Road, Hertfordshire WD2 4BX
0923 52075
WILLESDEN 473 High Road, London NW10 2JH
081 459 3989
WIMBLEDON 1 Weir Road, off Durnsford Road, London
SW19 081 946 9802
WORCESTER Hylton Road, Worcestershire WR2 5JW
0905 420401
WORLE North Worle District Centre, Queensway Road,
Weston-Super-Mare, Avon BS22 0BT 0934 512628
YORK Junction Monkgate/Foss Bank, North Yorkshire
YO3 7JB 0904 643911

FRANCE

PARIS ET REGION PARISIENNE
94 rue de Rennes 75006 Paris Tel (1) 45 48 43 89
95 avenue Raymond Poincaré 75016 Paris Tel (1) 45 01 24 73
261 rue Saint Honoré 75001 Paris Tel (1) 42 86 84 13
(shop and decorator showroom)
Galeries Lafayette 40 bld. Haussmann 75009 Paris 1em
étage, prêt-à-porter Tel (1) 42 82 34 56
5ème ètage, Décoration Tel (1) 42 82 04 11

AU PRINTEMPS
Nouveau Magasin 2ème étage 64 bld. Haussmann 75009
Paris Tel (1) 42 82 52 10 (Prêt-à-porter)
Le Printemps de la Maison 7ème étage Tel (1) 42 82 44 20
(Décoration)
Centre Commercial Vélizy 2 Avenue de l'Europe 78140
Vélizy Villacoublay
Niveau 2, (Prêt-à-porter) Tel (1) 39 46 96 85
Niveau 3, (Décoration) Tel (1) 39 56 87 66
Centre Commercial Parly 2 Avenue Charles de Gaulle
78150 Le Chesnay
Niveau 1, (Décoration) Tel (1) 39 54 22 44
Niveau 2, (Prêt-à-porter) Tel (1) 39 54 22 44

AIX EN PROVENCE 4 rue Joseph Cabassol Aix en
Provence Tel 42 27 31 92
BORDEAUX 2 place du Palais Bordeaux Tel 56 44 10 30
DIJON 18-20 rue Piron Dijon Tel 80 30 04 44
LILLE 25 rue de la Grande Chaussée Lille Tel 20 06 90 06
LYON 98 rue Président Edourd Herriot Lyon
Tel 78 37 18 19
NANCY 4 rue des Dominicains Nancy Tel 83 35 21 09
NANTES 16 rue Crébillon Nantes Tel 40 73 17 18
NICE Galeries Lafayette 2ème étage 6 avenue Jean Médecin
06000 Nice Tel 93 85 39 58
ROUEN 19 rue du Gros Horloge Rouen Tel 35 70 20 02
STRASBOURG 2 rue de Temple Neuf Strasbourg
Tel 88 75 18 19
TOULON Au Printemps, Centre Commercial 'Grand Var'
Avenue de l'Université Tel 94 21 89 58
TOULOUSE 50 rue Boulbonne Toulouse Tel 61 21 38 85

ITALY
MILAN Via Brera 4 20121 Milan Tel 02 80 84 77

AUSTRIA
SALZBURG Judengasse 11 Salzburg Tel 0662 84 03 44
VIENNA Weihburggasse 5 Vienna Tel 0222 512 93 12

NETHERLANDS
AMSTERDAM Leidsestraat 7 Amsterdam Tel 020 22 80 87
ARNHEM Bakkerstraat 17 Arnhem Tel 085 43 02 50
EINDHOVEN Demer 24a Eindhoven Tel 040 43 50 22
's-GRAVENHAGE Hoogstraat 32/Paleispromenade
's-Gravenhage Tel 070 3600540
MAASTRICHT Brugstraat 8 Maastricht Tel 043 25 09 72
ROTTERDAM Lijnbaan 63 Rotterdam Tel 010 414 85 35
UTRECHT Oudegracht 141 3511 Utrecht Tel 030 31 30 51

SWITZERLAND
BASEL Stadthausgasse 18 Tel 061 25 97 57
GENEVA 8 rue Verdine Tel 022 28 33 40
(Décoration) and 022 21 34 95 (Vêtements)
ZURICH Augustinergasse 21 Zurich Tel 01 221 13 94
BERN Marktgasse 2 Tel 031 21 06 96

GERMANY
FRANKFURT Goethestrasse 3 Frankfurt am Main
Tel 069 28 87 91/2
HAMBURG Neuer Wall 39 Hamburg
Tel 040 37 11 73/37 14 24
STUTTGART Breite Strasse 2 Stuttgart Tel 0711 226 10 64
HANOVER Georgstrasse 36 Hanover Tel 0511 32 69 19
DÜSSELDORF Hunsrückenstrasse 43 Düsseldorf
Tel 0211 32 70 09/0
MUNICH Sendlingerstrasse 37 Munich Tel 089 2606 82 24
BREMEN Sögestrasse 54 Bremen Tel 0421 17 04 43
COLOGNE Hohestrasse 160-168 Cologne Tel 0221 21 27 16
BERLIN (Im Kadewe) Tauentzienstrasse 21-24 Berlin
Tel 030 24 50 27
AACHEN Am Holzgraben 1-3 Aachen Tel 49 241 303
AUGSBERG Karlstrasse 15 Tel 49 08 21 17 71 88
BIELEFELD Niedernstrasse 14 Tel 49 05 21 17 71 88
WIESBADEN Langgasse 30 Tel 061 30 20 86
NUERNBERG Ludwigplatz 79 Tel 0911 24 518 19
MUENSTER Ludgeriestrasse 79 Tel 0251 42 272/73
KARLSRUHE Kaiserstrasse 104 Tel 0721 25 969

BELGIUM
ANTWERP Frankrijklei 27 Antwerp Tel 032 34 34 61
BRUSSELS 45 rue de Namur Brussels Tel 02 512 04 47
(Décoration) 81/83 rue de Namur Brussels Tel 02 512 86 39
(Vêtements)
GENT Volderstraat 15 Gent Tel 091 24 08 19

ASSOCIATED SHOPS
SWEDEN
STOCKHOLM Birger Stockholm Tel 08 102627
GOTHENBURG, Tel 031 115454, Arkaden Gothenburg
MALMO Skomokregatan 10 Malmo Tel 040 976100

NORWAY
OSLO Riddervoldsgate 10B Oslo 2 Tel 02 444030
BERGEN Engen 51 5000 Bergen Tel 05 901 836

DENMARK
COPENHAGEN Kompagnistaade 16 Copenhagen
Tel 0331 50306

GREECE
ATHENS 28 Herodotou Street 10673 Kolonaki Athens
Tel 030 7246869
ATHENS 18 Ioannou Metaxa Street Athens Tel 030
8944 400

ICELAND
REYKJAVIK Laugavegi 99 Reykjavik Tel 41 16646

FINLAND
HELSINKI Unioninkatu 32 Helsinki 10 Tel 0 6121466

ITALY
TURIN Via Andrea Dori 21/B 10123 Turin Tel 0 11 540295
FLORENCE Via Porta Rossa 56R Tel 055 311795
ROME Piazza S Lorenzo in Lucina 2 Rome Tel 06 6871395
ROME Vigola Bella Torretta 2 Rome Tel 06 6871158
NAPLES Via Rampe Brancaccio 5 Naples Tel 081 5108563
CAGLIARI SARDINIA Via Dante 69/C 09100 Cagliari
Tel 070 485075
PALERMO SICILY 19 Via G. Daita Palermo Tel 091 585403
VERONA Via E. Noris 6/B Verona Tel 045 8002427

SPAIN
TENERIFE Sabino Betherlot 4 Tenerife Tel 020 275905

PORTUGAL
LISBON Praca De Londres 8-8c Lisbon Tel 011 678351

HONG KONG
HONG KONG Shop 223-225 2nd Floor Princes Building Hong Kong Tel 5245041

SOUTH KOREA
SEOUL P.O. Box 344 Tel 02 25496701

MEXICO
MEXICO
Periferico Sur 3335, C.P. 10200 Tel (5) 6837433
Centro Comercial Interlomas Q-2, C.P. 52760 Tel (5) 2511539

UNITED STATES OF AMERICA
ALABAMA
BIRMINGHAM-HOOVER Riverchase Galleria Mall 35244 Tel (205) 985-0090
MONTGOMERY 2769 Montgomery Mall East South Blvd. 36116 Tel (205) 284-7011

ARIZONA
PHOENIX Biltmore Fashion Park 85016 Tel (602) 956-6043

ARKANSAS
LITTLE ROCK 3016 Park Plaza Mall 72205 Tel (501) 666-0272

CALIFORNIA
CARMEL BY THE SEA Carmel Plaza 93921 Tel (408) 624-8095
CENTURY CITY Shopping Center 10250 Santa Monica Blvd. Los Angeles 90067 Tel (213) 533-0807
CORTE MADERA The Village at Corte Madera 94925 Tel (415) 924-5770
COSTA MESA South Coast Plaza 92626 Tel (714) 545-9322
GLENDALE 2153 Glendale Galleria 91210 Tel (818) 242-0428
LA JOLLA 7852 Girard Avenue 92037 Tel (619) 459-3733
BEVERLY CENTER 121 N. La Cienega Boulevard Los Angeles 90048 Tel (213) 854-0490
PALM SPRINGS Desert Fashion Mall 92262 Tel (619) 322-2099
PALO ALTO 12 Stanford Shopping Center 94304 Tel (415) 328-0560
BULLOCKS PASADENA 401 S. Lake Avenue 91101 Tel (818) 792-0211
PLEASANTON 2651 Stoneridge Mall 94588
REDONDO BEACH The Galleria at South Bay 90278 Tel (213) 542-4436
SACRAMENTO 531 Pavilions Lane 95825 Tel (916) 923-5696
SAN DIEGO 247 Horton Plaza 92101 Tel (619) 234-0663
SAN DIEGO 4505 La Jolla Village Drive 92122 Tel (619) 452-6116
SAN JOSE/SANTA CLARA Valley Fair Mall 95050 Tel (408) 224-3551
SAN FRANCISCO 1827 Union Street 94123 Tel (415) 922-7200
SAN FRANCISCO 253 Post Street 94108 Tel (415) 788-0190
SANTA ANNA Mainplace 2800 North Main Street 92701 Tel (714) 834-1211
SANTA BARBARA 3891 State Street 93105 Tel (805) 682-8878
WALNUT CREEK 1171 Broadway Plaza 94596 Tel (415) 947-5920
BULLOCKS WESTWOOD 10861 Weyburn Ave. 90025 Tel (213) 208-4211
WOODLAND HILLS 279 Promenade Mall 91367 Tel (818) 346-7560

COLORADO
BOULDER 1136 Pearl Street 80302 Tel (303) 938-1511
DENVER 1439 Larimer Street 80202 Tel (303) 571-0050

CONNECTICUT
DANBURY Danbury Fair Mall 06810 Tel (203) 790-5068
GREENWICH 321 Greenwich Avenue 06830 Tel (203) 661-5678
FARMINGTON-HARTFORD 294 West Farms Mall New Canaan Farmington 06032 Tel (203) 521-8967
NEW CANAAN 124 Elm Street 06840 Tel (203) 966-5509
NEW HAVEN 260-262 College Street 06510 Tel (203) 782-9436

STAMFORD Stamford Town Center 06901 Tel (203) 324-1067
WESTPORT 85 Main Street 06880 Tel (203) 226-7495

DELAWARE
WILMINGTON 4009 Kennett Pike Greenville 19807 Tel (302) 575-1653

FLORIDA
BAL HARBOUR 9700 Collins Avenue 33154 Tel (305) 864-5628
BOCA RATON 80 Town Center Mall 33431 Tel (407) 368-5622
FORT LAUDERDALE Galleria Mall 33304 Tel (305) 563-2300
JACKSONVILLE The Jacksonville Landing 32202 Tel (904) 358-7548
MIAMI The Falls 33176 Tel (305) 233-8911
ORLANDO 290 Park Avenue North Winter Park 32779 Tel (407) 740-8900
PALM BEACH 320 Worth Avenue 33480 Tel (407) 832-3188
PALM BEACH GARDENS The Gardens 3101 PGA Blvd 33410 Tel (407) 624-5901
TAMPA 718 South Village Circle Old Hyde Park Village 33606 Tel (813) 253-2177

GEORGIA
ATLANTA Lenox Square 30326 Tel (404) 231-0685
ATLANTA Perimeter Mall 30346 Tel (404) 395-6027
SAVANNAH Oglethorpe Mall 31416 Tel (912) 355-7704

HAWAII
HONOLULU 1450 Ala Moana Center 96814 Tel (808) 942-5200

ILLINOIS
CHICAGO Watertower Place 60611 Tel (312) 951-8004
LAKE FOREST 272 Market Square 60045 Tel (708) 615-1405
NORTHBROOK Northbrook Court 60062 Tel (708) 480-1660
OAKBROOK 224 Oakbrook Center 60521 Tel (708) 572-9195
OLD ORCHARD SKOKIE Old Orchard Shopping Center 60077 Tel (708) 673-6604
WOODFIELD Woodfield Mall Schaumburg 60173 Tel (708) 619-9110

INDIANA
INDIANAPOLIS Fashion Mall 46240 Tel (317) 848-9855

IOWA
DES MOINES Kaleidoscope at the Hub 50309 Tel (515) 243-8881

KENTUCKY
LEXINGTON Victorian Square 401 West Main Street 40507 Tel (606) 253-1724
LOUISVILLE Louisville Galleria 40202 Tel (502) 585 2424

LOUISIANA
KENNER The Esplanade 70065 Tel (504) 465-0213
NEW ORLEANS 333 Canal Place 70130 Tel (504) 522-9403

MAINE
FREEPORT 58-60 Main Street 04032 Tel (207) 865-3300

MARYLAND
ANNAPOLIS 139 Main Street 21401 Tel (301) 268-6906
BALTIMORE Pratt Street Pavilion 201 East Pratt Street 21202 Tel (301) 539-0500
OWINGS MILLS Owings Mill Town Center 21117 Tel (301) 363-2455
NORTH BETHESDA WHITE FLINT White Flint Mall 20895 Tel (301) 984-3223

MASSACHUSETTS
BOSTON 82 Newbury Street 02116 Tel (617) 536-0505
BURLINGTON Burlington Mall 01803 Tel (617) 272-4540
CAMBRIDGE Charles Square 02138 Tel (617) 576-3690
CHESTNUT HILL The Mall at Chestnut Hill 02167 Tel (617) 965-7640
HINGHAM 66 South Street 02043 Tel (617) 740-4122

OHIO
BEACHWOOD 203 Beachwood Place 26300 Cedar Road 44122 Tel (216) 831 7621
CINCINNATI Kenwood Towne Center 45236 Tel (713) 793-5535
CLEVELAND 342 Galleria Tower Erieview 44114 Tel (216) 579-1301
COLUMBUS 342 Columbus City Center Drive 43215 Tel (614) 224-5057
DAYTON Shops of Oakwood 2426 Far Hills Avenue 45419 Tel (513) 299-9007
COLUMBUS/WORTHINGTON 108 Worthington Square 43085 Tel (614) 433-9011

OKLAHOMA
TULSA 1846 Utica Square 74114 Tel (918) 749-5001

OREGON
PORTLAND 419 S.W. Morrison Street 97204 Tel (503) 224-0703

PENNSYLVANIA
ARDMORE 29 On the Square 19003 Tel (215) 896-0208
GERMANTOWN 8520 Germantown Avenue Chestnut Hill 19118 Tel (215) 242-9262
KING OF PRUSSIA Court at King of Prussia 338 Goddard Blvd. 19406 Tel (215) 354-3130
PHILADELPHIA 1721 Walnut Street 19103 Tel (215) 496-0492
PITTSBURG Station Square 15219 Tel (412) 391-7993
PITTSBURG 1000 Ross Part Mall 15237 Tel (412) 367-8881
PITTSBURG SHADY SIDE Hartwell Building 5401 Walnut Street 15232 Tel (412) 621-0735

RHODE ISLAND
NEWPORT 18 Bowen's Wharf America's Cup Avenue 02840 Tel (401) 846-6980
PROVIDENCE 2 Davol Square Mall 02903 Tel (401) 273-1120

SOUTH CAROLINA
CHARLESTON Charleston Place 146 Market Street 29401 Tel (803) 723-3967
MYRTLE BEACH Outlet Park at Waccaman 29577 Tel (803) 236-4244

TENNESSEE
CHATTANOOGA Hamilton Place Mall 37421 Tel (615) 855-5496
MEMPHIS GERMANTOWN Saddle Creek Shopping Center 38138 Tel (901) 756-7036
KNOXVILLE Melrose Place 37919 Tel (615) 558-6358
NASHVILLE The Mall at Green Hills 37215 Tel (615) 383-0131

TEXAS
AUSTIN Highland Mall 6001 Airport Blvd. 78752 Tel (512) 451-4036
DALLAS 13350 Dallas Parkway Galleria 75240 Tel (214) 980-9858
DALLAS 423 North Park Center 75225 Tel (214) 369-5755
FORT WORTH 213 Hulen Mall 76132 Tel (817) 346-4666
HOUSTON Galleria 5015 Westheimer 77056 Tel (713) 871-9669
HOUSTON 1000 West Oaks Mall 77082 Tel (713) 558-6113
PLANO 2100 Collin Creek Mall 75075 Tel (214) 578-8600
SAN ANTONIO North Star Mall 78216 Tel (512) 377-2833

UTAH
SALT LAKE CITY 267 Trolley Square 84102 Tel (801) 363-8408

VERMONT
BURLINGTON 23 Church Street 05401 Tel (802) 658-5006

VIRGINIA
ARLINGTON Pentagon City 1100 South Hayes Street 22202 Tel (703) 415-2111
CHARLOTTESVILLE Barracks Road Shopping Center 22901 Tel (804) 971-7707
FAIR OAKS 11822 Fair Oaks Mall Fairfax 22033 Tel (703) 352-7960
McLEAN Tyson's Corner Center 1961 Chain Bridge Road 22102 Tel (703) 827-0074

PRINCE WILLIAM 2700 Potomac Mills Circle 22192
Tel (703) 494-3124
REGENCY SQUARE Regency Square Mall, Richmond
23229 Tel (804) 740-1406
RICHMOND Commercial Block 23219 Tel (804) 644-1050
WILLIAMSBURG Merchants Square 23185 Tel (804) 229-0353

WASHINGTON
SEATTLE 405 University Street 98101 Tel (206) 343-9637

WASHINGTON D.C.
WASHINGTON 3213 M Street N.W. Georgetown 20007
Tel (202) 338-5481
WASHINGTON Chevy Chase Pavillion 5345 Wisconsin
Avenue 20015

WISCONSIN
MILWAUKEE The Grand Avenue 53203 Tel (414) 347-1930

MOTHER & CHILD SHOPS
AUSTIN Highland Mall Texas 78752 Tel (512) 452 2536
BEACHWOOD 124 Beachwood Place Ohio 44122
Tel (216) 591 0192
BIRMINGHAM Galleria Mall Alabama 35244 Tel (205)
987 7566
BRIDGEWATER Bridgewater Commons Mall New Jersey
08807 Tel (201) 704 8700
CHARLOTTE Southpark Shopping Center North Carolina
28211 Tel (704) 364 4093
CHERRY CREEK Shopping Center Denver Colorado
80208 Tel (303) 322 9403
CHESTNUT HILL The Mall Maine 02167 Tel (617) 965 5687
CHEVY CHASE Pavillion Washington DC 20015
CINCINNATI Kenwood Towne Center Ohio 45236
Tel (513) 791 5371
COSTA MESA 3333 Bristol Street California 92626
Tel (714) 546 1112
DALLAS 216 North Park Center Texas 75225 Tel (214)
373 9381
FAIRFAX Fair Oaks Mall Virginia 22033 Tel (703) 273 9861
HARTFORD 279 West Farms Mall Connecticut 06032
Tel (203) 561 4870
HOUSTON-GALLERIA 5015 Westheimer Texas 77056
Tel (713) 622 2262
KANSAS CITY Country Club Plaza Missouri 64112
Tel (816) 931 2810
KING OF PRUSSIA 338 Goddard Boulevard Pennsylvania
19406 Tel (215) 354 9137
MEMPHIS Saddlecreek Shopping Center Tennessee 38138
Tel (901) 753 7053
NEW ORLEANS Canal Place Mall Louisiana 70130 Tel (504)
586 8652
PALM BEACH GARDENS The Gardens Florida 33410
Tel (407) 624 5905
PRINCETON 39 Palmer Square West New Jersey 08542
Tel (609) 683 1300
REDONDO BEACH Galleria South Bay California 90278
Tel (213) 542 6228
RIVERSIDE SQUARE 257 Riverside Square Mall Hackensack
New Jersey 07601 Tel (201) 342 1222
SHORT HILLS The Mall New Jersey 07078 Tel (201)
564 9600
STAMFORD Town Center Connecticut 06901 Tel (203)
359 9902
TROY Somerset Fashion Mall Michigan 48084 Tel (313)
649 0880
TULSA 1846 Utica Square Oklahoma 74114 Tel (918)
749 5063
WALNUT CREEK 1163 Broadway Plaza California 94596
Tel (415) 947 3932
WHITE FLINT White Flint Mall 20895 Tel (301) 230 0081
WOODFIELD Woodfield Mall Illinois 60173 Tel (708)
240 1910

HOME STORES
ALEXANDRIA 821 S. Washington Street Virginia 22314
Tel (703) 739 2144
ARDMORE 42 Saint James Place Pennsylvania 19003
Tel (215) 896 8293
BUCKHEAD 1 West Paces Ferry Road Atlanta Georgia
30305
BURLINGAME 1375 Burlingame Avenue California 94010

Tel (415) 344 1774
CHEVY CHASE Mazza Galleria Washington DC 20015
Tel (202) 686 1200
COSTA MESA South Coast Plaza California 92626 Tel (714)
545 7927
KANSAS CITY 308 West 47th Street Missouri 64112
Tel (816) 531 8971
NEW YORK 714 Madison Avenue New York 10021
Tel (212) 735 5000
NORTH PARK 612 Northpark Center Dallas Texas 75225
Tel (214) 691 6871
RIDGEWOOD 171 E. Ridgewood Avenue New Jersey
07451 Tel (201) 670 0868

CANADA
BAYVIEW Shopping Center 2901 Bayview Avenue
Willowdale Ontario M2K 1E6 Tel (416) 223-9507
CALGARY-ALBERTA Banker's Hall-Suite 315 8th Avenue
S.W. Tel (403) 269 4090
LONDON ONTARIO Galleria London 355 Wellington
Street Tel (519) 434 1703
MONTREAL 2110 Crescent Street Quebec H3G 2B8
Tel (514) 284-9225
OTTAWA 136 Bank Street Ontario K1P 5N8 Tel (613) 238-4882
SHERWAY GARDENS-ETOBICOKE 25 The West Mall
Ontario Tel (416) 620 7222
STE. FOY 2452 Blvd. Wilfred Laurier Quebec Tel (418) 659
6660
TORONTO 18 Hazelton Avenue Ontario M5R 2E2
Tel (416) 922-7761
TORONTO-YORKDALE Yorkdale Shopping Center 3401
(Dufferin Street Ontario Tel (416) 256 2040
VANCOUVER 1171 Robson St. British Colombia V6E 1B5
Tel (604) 688-8729
WINNIPEG Portage Place–393 Portage Avenue Manitoba
Tel (204) 943 3093

AUSTRALIA
MELBOURNE 97 Elizabeth Street Victoria 3000
Tel 602 2962
MELBOURNE Laura Ashley at David Jones Bourke Street
Victoria 3000 Tel 655 1680 (Home Furnishings only)
ARMADALE 1036 High Street Victoria 3143 Tel 509 3365
CAMBERWELL 781 Burke Road Victoria 3124 Tel 882 3986
DONCASTER 69 Doncaster Shoppingtown Victoria 3108
Tel 840 1487
GEELONG 49 Market Square Victoria 3220 Tel 21 3709
RICHMOND 236 Swan Street Victoria 3121 Tel 427 9268
SOUTH MELBOURNE 462 City Road Victoria 3205
Tel 690 9666 (Home Furnishings only)
SOUTHLAND 287 Southland Shopping Centre Cheltenham
Victoria 3192 Tel 583 9750
SYDNEY 114 Castlereagh Street New South Wales 2000
Tel 261 2458
SYDNEY Centrepoint Castlereagh Street New South
Wales 2000 Tel 232 2829
CHATSWOOD The Gallery Lemon Grove New South
Wales 2067 Tel 419 5352
CHATSWOOD Laura Ashley at David Jones New South
Wales 2067 Tel 411 9113 (Home Furnishings only)
DARLING HARBOUR Shop 353-355 Sydney New South
Wales 2000 Tel 281 4091
DARLINGHURST 40 Oxford Street New South Wales
2010 Tel 361 3846
DOUBLE BAY 3 Transvaal Avenue New South Wales 2028
Tel 327 1799
MOSMAN 1-3 Mandalong Road New South Wales 2088
Tel 968 1314
NORTH RYDE 12 Macquarie Shopping Centre New South
Wales 2113 Tel 805 0665
ADELAIDE The Gallerie Shopping Centre Gawler Place
South Australia 5000 Tel 223 6548
BRISBANE Shop 181 Myer Centre Queen Street
Queensland 4000 Tel 229 3928
CANBERRA Shop G49 Woden Plaza 2601 ACT
Tel 285 2378
CANBERRA Laura Ashley at David Jones Civic 2600 ACT
Tel 274 3309 (Home Furnishings only)
HOBART Centrepoint 209 Murray Street Tasmania 7000
Tel 34 3484
PERTH City Arcade Hay Street Level Western Australia
6000 Tel 321 2391

TOKYO
GINZA 6-10-12 Ginza Chuo-Ku 104 Tel (03) 3571 5011
AOYAMA Honey Bldg 3-35-8, Jingumae, Shibuya-Ku 150
Tel (03) 5474 5011
KICHIJOJI 2-4-14, Kichijoji Honcho, Musashino-Shi 180
Tel (0422) 21 1203
JIYUGAOKA 1-26-18, Jiyugaoka, Meguro-Ku 152 Tel (03)
3724 0051
SHIBUYA Proto Bldg., 12-17, Udagawa-Cho, Shibuya-Ku
150 Tel (03) 3464 5011
NAGOYA-Sugi Bldg., 3-14-15 Sakae, Naka-Ku, Nagoya-Shi
460 Tel (052) 262 5011
HIROSHIMA 8-32, Hondori, Naka-Ku, Hiroshima-Shi 730
Tel (082) 247 5011
KURAKUEN Dekolashion Bldg. 1F & 2F, 15-1, Minami-
Koshikiiwa-Cho, Nishinomiya-Shi 662 Tel (0798) 72 0336

SHOP-IN-SHOPS
TOKYO
NIHONBASHI MITSUKOSHI 1-4-1, Nihonbashi
Muromachi, Chuo-Ku 103 Tel (03) 3241 5617
SHINJUKU MITSUKOSHI 3-29-1, Shinjuku, Shinjuku-Ku
160 Tel (03) 3225 7389
GINZA MITSUKOSHI 4-6-16, Ginza, Chuo-Ku 104 Tel (03)
3561 4050
IKEBUKURO MITSUKOSHI 1-5-7, Higashi-Ikebukuro,
Toshima-Ku 170 Tel (03) 3987 6074
TOKYU HONTEN 2-24-1 Dogenzaka, Shibuya-Ku 150
Tel (03) 3477 3836
SHINJUKU KEIO 1-1-4, Nishi Shinjuku, Shinjuku-Ku 160
Tel (03) 3344 0080
FUTAKO TAMAGAWA (Tamagawa Takashimaya Shopping
Centre) 3-17-1, Tamagawa, Setagaya-Ku 158 Tel (03)
3708 3151
TAMA SOGO 1-46-1, Ochiai, Tama-Shi 206 Tel (0423)
339 2450

KANAGAWA PREFECTURE
YOKOHAMA MITSUKOSHI 1-2-7, Kita Saiwai, Nishi-Ku,
Yokohama-Shi 220 Tel (045) 322 2144
YOKOHAMA PRINCE HOTEL 3-13-1, Isogo, Isogo-Ku,
Yokohama-Shi 235 Tel (045) 754 4655
KAWASAKI SAIKAYA 1 Ogawa-Cho, Kawasaki-Ku,
Kawasaki-Shi 210 Tel (044) 211 8581
YOKOSUKA SAIKAYA 1-10, Ootaki-Cho, Yokosuka-Shi
238 Tel (0468) 23 1234

CHIBA PREFECTURE
CHIBA MITSUKOSHI 2-6-1 Fujimi, Chiba-Shi 280
Tel (0472) 27 4731

NORTHERN JAPAN
BANDAI MITSUKOSHI 1-3-30, Bandai, Niigata-Shi 950
Tel (025) 243 6333
KORINBO 109 2-1-1, Korinbo, Kanazawa-Shi 920
Tel (0762) 20 5226
SAPPORO TOKYU 2-1, Shijyo-Nishi, Kita, Chyo-Ku,
Sapporo-Shi 060 Tel (011) 212 2658

KANSAI AREA
ABENO KINTETSU 1-1-43, Abenosuji, Abeno-Ku, Osaka-
Shi 545 Tel (06) 625 2332
KOBE SOGO 8-1-8, Onoe-Dori, Chuo-Ku, Kobe-Shi 651
Tel (078) 242 5100
UMEDA HANKYU 8-7, Sumida-Cho, Kita-Ku, Osaka-Shi
530 Tel (06) 365 0793
KAWANISHI HANKYU 26-1, Sakae-Cho, Kawanishi-Shi
666 Tel (0727) 56 1622
HIROSHIMA MITSUKOSHI 5-1, Ebishu-Cho, Naka-Ku,
Hiroshima-Shi 730 Tel (082) 241 5055
HAKATA IZUTSUYA 1-1, Chuo-Gai, Hakata-Eki, Hakata-
Ku, Fukuoka-Shi 812 Tel (092) 452 2181
FUKUOKA TAMAYA 3-7-30, Nakasu, Hakata-Ku, Fukuoka-
Shi 812 Tel (092) 271 6580
NAGOYA MITSUKOSHI 3-5-1, Sakae, Naka-Ku, Nagoya-
Shi 460 Tel (052) 252 1838
SEISHIN SOGO 5-9-4, Koujidai, Nishi-Ku, Kobe-Shi 673
Tel (078) 992 1586
GIFU MELSA 1-15, Tetsumei-Dori, Gifu-Shi 500 Tel (0582)
66 3136

All addresses correct at time of going to press

PHOTOGRAPHIC ACKNOWLEDGEMENTS

Arcaid 26 bottom, 27 (Richard Bryant), 31 top, 32, 35, 76 and 83 (Richard Bryant); Laura Ashley 17 bottom, 37, 38, 45 top, 60 top, 62 top, 67, 69 top, 70, 71, 73 top and bottom, 74, 75, 79, 81 top, 84 bottom, 85, 88 top, 89 right; Michael Boys Syndication 13 bottom, 22; The Bridgeman Art Library 24; Andreas Einseidel 23 bottom; Michael Freeman 10, 28 top, 29; Lars Hallén 25 top; Robert Harding Picture library 11, 14 bottom, 15, 19, 30, 31 bottom, 34 top, 40, 41, 42 top, 46, 47 top, 51 left, 59, 60 bottom, 63 top and bottom, 64 top and bottom, 68 left, 72, 78 bottom, 80, 81 bottom, 84 top, 86, 87, 88 bottom, 90 top and bottom, 91 top (Gwenan Murphy), 92 top and bottom, 93; Lorrie Mack 36 (Shona Wood), 45 bottom, 61 top (Bill Strites); Ianthe Ruthven 12, 13 top, 14 top, 17 top, 20 left, 21 top and bottom, 43, 44, 47 bottom, 48, 50, 51 right, 52, 53, 58, 77, 82, 89 top, 91 bottom; Paul Ryan 26 top, 33, 78 top, 89 left; Fritz von der Schulenberg 8, 20 right, 28 bottom, 61 left, 66; Elizabeth Whiting & Associates 18, 23 top, 25 bottom, 34 bottom, 42 bottom, 49, 62 bottom, 65, 68 right.

All other photographs © George Weidenfeld and Nicolson Ltd

In addition the publishers would like to thank the following: Roderick James, Architect, Carpenter Oak and Woodland Company, Chippenham, Wiltshire for loaning us his Studio Barn for jacket photography, and his wife, Gillie James, who made the patchwork quilt; Sinclair Till, 791–3 Wandsworth Road, London SW8; Fired Earth, Middle Aston Oxon and Crucial Trading PO Box 689, London W8 4BX for loaning flooring materials; Maggie Hadden for making the rag rug and Diane Hadden for making the cushions; Bill and Julia James; Lizzie and James Staples; Liz Woodhouse; Pavilion Antiques, Freshford; Pia Tryde; and Spriggs Florists, Petworth for assisting in the section on 'Accessorizing the Country Look'.

INDEX

Figures in **bold** refer to illustration captions

air fresheners 51
airers, clothes 63
alcoves, fireplace **79**
American styles:
  Colonial 26–7
  Shaker 29
anemones **154**, **161**
antiquing (painting technique) **99**, 100
  on chairs 112, **112**, **113**
appliqué designs for cushions 138, **138**
architraves, painting 46
armoires 18, **19**
artichokes, globe **156**
attic bedrooms **80**

bags:
  making draw-string 133, **133**
  making hold-all 140, **140**
barns, converted *see* conversions
baseboards *see* skirtings
basins 87, **87**
  bedroom 80
baskets **20**, 65, 153
  clothes 63
  for flowers and plants 74, 161
  log **46**, 73–4
  for office use **71**
  for storage 85, **162**, **163**
bath essence, lavender **177**
bathrooms **14**, **36**, **50**, 87, **87**, **88**
  baths **21**, 87
  floors 87
  lighting 52
  walls 87, **87**, 89, **89**
  white **89**
bay 172, **172**
beams, timber 16, **17**, 46
  bleaching **47**
bedlinen **50**, 80
  lace 132, **132**, **133**
  striped **78**
bedrooms **14**, **20**, **21**, **22**, **26**, 77
  basins in 80
  floor coverings 48
  storage 77
  wardrobes and chests 79
  see also bedlinen; beds
beds:
  brass **81**
  children's 85
  coverlets for **14**, **21**, **57**, **78**, 80;
    see also quilts
  four-poster **26**, **77**, **81**
  headboards for **57**, 77

pencil-post 27
positioning of 77
sleigh 77
truckle or trundle 27, 85
Tuscan (iron) **44**
valances for 80
berries **183**, **184**
  dried **159**
birds' nests **189**
blackberries **171**
blinds, roller and venetian 49
boxes:
  collections of **186**
  Shaker **28**, 29
bulbs, for indoors **168**, 168–9, **169**
bump 15

candles **52**, **67**, **68**, **69**, **184**
  displaying **160**
  holders for 184, **184**
  sconces **20**, **69**, **75**
cane furniture 49
  chairs **49**, **54**, 72, **93**
  tables **189**
ceilings 41
  low 41
  sloping 42, **43**
centrepieces, table **31**, **68**, **156**, **183**, **183**, **184**, **184**
chairs:
  antiquing 112, **112**, **113**
  cane **49**, **54**, 72, **93**
  comb-back **69**
  cushion for kitchen chair 134, **134**
  dining **67**, 72
  ladderback **17**, **29**, **67**, **68**
  loose covers for 71, 72
  occasional 72
  Provençal **18**
  rocking **11**, 25, 27, 72
  steel **33**
  stick-back **48**; *see also* Windsor
  tilter 29
  upholstered **13**, 71, **72**, **74**, **75**
  verdigris finishing for 106, **107**
  Windsor **26**, **71**, **75**
chamber pots **50**
cheese, goat's **172**
chestnuts, sweet **171**
children's rooms 82
  beds 85
  floor coverings 82, **84**, 85
  furniture **83**, **84**, 84, 85
  storage **83**, **85**, 85, 108, **108**
  wallpaper **83**, **84**

chillies **156**
  dried 31, **31**, **159**
chintz 15, **56**
Chintz (Laura Ashley Collection) 128–9, **128–9**
Christmas garlands, making 164, **164**
cladding, timber *see* timber cladding
clematis, wild **150**, **157**
clothes airer, overhead 63
clothes basket 63
coffee tables 72–3
coffer, oak **17**
coir matting 15, 48, **49**, 81, 120, **120**
collections 153, **161**, 170, 186, **186**, 189, **189**
  displaying **13**, **153**, **163**
Colonial style 26–7
Coloured Woven Jacquard (Laura Ashley
    Collection) 130, **130**
colours 11
  size of rooms and 41
  strong **41**, 42
  temperature and 42
colourwashing (painting technique) 46, 96, **96**
conservatories **19**, 92–3
conversions **21**, **34**, 35–6, **35**, **36**
cork flooring 59
cornices 41
cotton fabrics:
  giving faded appearance to 50
  Laura Ashley Collection 128–31, **128–31**
  Provençal **19**, **19**
  PVC-coated **19**, 60, 64, 129, **129**
Country Furnishing Cotton (Laura
    Ashley Collection) 128, **128**
Country Linen Union (Laura Ashley
    Collection) 129, **129**
country houses 14–15
coverlets **14**, **21**, **57**, 80; *see also* quilts
crockery 65, **186**
crystallizing flower petals 174, **175**
cup and saucer collections **13**, 153, **186**
cupboards:
  armario **31**
  armoires 18, **19**
  corner **194**
  kitchen 59–60, **60**, 61, **61**
curtains 15, 48–9
  café 26
  cottage 16, **16**
  cotton lace 49
  door **90**
  fabrics for 128–31, **128–31**
  Mediterranean 22
  Morris design **17**
  Provençal 19

quilts as 16, **54**
shower 87, 89
Swedish 24
Tuscan 21
cushions 30, 48, **72**, 73
adding braid or fringing to 135, **135**
appliqué designs for 138, **138**
fabrics for 128–31, **128–31**
making bedroom 80
making for kitchen chair 134, **134**
making rectangular 140, **140**

daffodils 154, **154**
daisies, Michaelmas **162**
dining rooms 19, **25**, 33, 35
floors 67
lighting 68, **68**, **69**
storage 67
see also table centrepieces
doors:
kitchen (swing) 62
stable **63**
stripped **73**
woodgraining 116, **116**, **117**
dragging (painting technique) **96**, 98
Drawing Room Fabric (Laura Ashley
Collection) 128, **128**
drawing rooms *see* living rooms
draw-string bags, making 133, **133**
dressers 61, 67, **195**
dressing tables 79

eggs, blown **189**
elderberries 170
elderflowers 170
encaustic tiles **119**
essence, lavender **177**

fabrics: Laura Ashley Collection:
Chintz 128–9, **128–9**
Coloured Woven Jacquard 130, **130**
Country Furnishing Cotton 128, **128**
Country Linen Union 129, **129**
Drawing Room Fabric 128, **128**
Lace 128, **128**
Lining Fabric 129, **129**
Ottoman 130, **130**
Plastic-Coated Fabric 129, **129**
Satin Weave 131, **131**
Ticking 131, **131**
Traditional Cotton 130–1, **130–1**
Upholstery Fabric 131, **131**
Voile 129, **129**
Woven Check 130, **130**
Woven Jacquard 131, **131**
see also soft furnishings
fireplaces **13**, 33, 51
bedroom 77
tiling around 122, **122**, 123
firescreen, making a 142, **142**
flagstone, Peruvian **119**

floorboards 121, **121**
painting 16, **46**, 48
chequered pattern 124, **124**, **125**
à la Matisse 125, **126**, **127**
stencilling 27, 50, 97, **97**
varnishing 16, 48
floors and floor coverings 33, 34, 43–4
American Colonial 26
bathroom 87
brick **35**
in children's rooms 82, **84**, 85
cork 59
cottage 16
country-house 14–15
floating 121, **121**
hard-wearing 46, 48
kitchen 59, **62**
linoleum 118, **118**
marble 119, **119**
marbling 101, **101**
mats and matting **36**, 48, **49**, 67, **73**, 120,
120
Mediterranean 22
parquet 121, **121**
Provençal 18
slate 119, **119**
stone 119, **119**
strip 121, **121**
Swedish 24
tiled **42**, 119, **119**
timber 121, **121**; *see also* floorboards
Tuscan 21
flowers 11, 51, **51**, 150, **150**
arrangements 68, 154, **154–7**, **162**, 163,
163
crystallizing petals **175**
for cutting 154
lotions from **175**
see also centrepieces, table; roses
fluorescent lighting 52
frames, spattering 102, **102**, **103**
Franklin, Benjamin 27
frescoes **20**
fruit arrangements **156**, 158, **158**
furniture 48, 49
American Colonial **26**, 26–7, **69**
cane 49, **49**, **54**, 72, **189**
cottage 16–17, **17**
country-house 15
Lloyd Loom 49–50
marbling 101, **101**
Mediterranean 22
mixing styles of 33–4, **34**
painting 21, 46, **65**
polish for 51, **177**
Provençal 18, **18**
ragging (painting technique) 97–8, **99**
Santa Fé style 30, **31**
Shaker **28**, 29, **29**, 46, 49
spattering (painting technique) 99, **101**
sponging (painting technique) 96–7, **98**

stencilling 27, 50, 97, **97**
Swedish 24–5, **25**
Tuscan 21
see also specific items

garden rooms 92–3
gardens 150, 153
garden sheds: storage systems 199, **199**
garlands **163**
Christmas 164, **164**
see also wreaths
guest bedrooms 77

halls **13**, **90**, 90–1, **91**
table displays 191
Tuscan style **20**
hearths, tiling 122, **122**, 123
heating 51–2
underfloor 51
see also stoves
herbs 65, 150, 153, 172, **172**
bouquets 173
sachets **173**
hold-all, making a 140, **140**
hops, sachets of **173**
hyacinths 154, 169, **169**
planting **168**
hydrangeas, drying **161**

jars, storage 64, 197
jasmine 89, **161**, 167
sachets **173**
jelly, apple **172**

kelim rugs **92**, 93
kitchens 13, **16**, **23**, **42**, **45**, 59
chair cushions 134, **134**
containers 64, **196**, 197, **197**
cupboards 59–60, **60**, 61, **61**, 62, **63**, **64**
doors (swing) 62
electrical appliances 59
floors 59
lighting 52
overhead racks 63, 65
pots and pans 63–4
shelves 60–1, **61**, **64**, 195, **195**
sinks 59
tables 61
walls 59, **60**
work surfaces 59

Lace (Laura Ashley Collection) 128, **128**
lace:
Chinese cutwork **81**
curtains 49, **49**
edging pillowcases with 132, **132**
nightdress case 132, **133**
pillowcase 132, **133**

lacquering, faux **100**, 101
    table 114, **114**, **115**
lamps 52, 75
    shades for 75
    sponging base of 104, **104**, **105**
Lancaster, Nancy 50
Larsson, Carl 24, **74**, **79**
    Watering the Plants 24
lavatory brush container 89
lavender 19, 172, 176
    bath essence **177**
    'bottles' 176, **176**
    as decoration **177**
    polish **177**
    posy **150**
    sachets 80, **173**
    wreaths 176, **176**
lighting 52
    dining room 68, **68**, **69**
    living room **25**, 75, **75**
    see also candles; lamps
limestone floors **119**
linen:
    Country Linen Union 129, **129**
    giving faded appearance to 50
    see also bedlinen
Lining Fabric (Laura Ashley Collection) 129, **129**
linoleum 59, **62**, 118
    tiles **118**
living rooms (drawing rooms; sitting rooms) **15**,
    17, **26**, **33**, **34**, **36**, **72**
    floors 48, 71
    lighting 75, **75**
    shelving in 73
    Swedish **25**
Lloyd Loom furniture 49–50
log containers 17, **46**, 73–4
loose covers 71, 72
    washing 71
lotions, home-made 175

marble:
    tiles **119**
    travertino **21**
marbling (painting technique) 101, **101**
matchboarding *see* tongue-and-grooved
    cladding
mats and matting:
    coir 48, **49**, 120, **120**
    medieval 120, **120**
    rush **36**, 48, 67, **73**
    seagrass 48, 120, **120**
    sisal 48, 120, **120**
Mediterranean style 22
medlars **171**
mimosa **154**
mirrors 87, 91, **92**, 192
mistletoe **157**
modern country style 33–4
Morris, William: 'Strawberry Thief'
    design **17**

napkins 68
    making 134, **134**
needlework samplers 27, **27**, 75
nerine bowdenii **157**
nightdress case, making 132, **133**

old man's beard **150**, **157**
Ottoman (Laura Ashley Collection) 130, **130**
ottomans 72
oven gloves, making 135, **135**

painting techniques:
    antiquing **99**, 100
    colourwashing 96, **96**
    dragging **96**, 98
    faux lacquering **100**, 101
    marbling 101, **101**
    ragging 97–8, **99**
    spattering 99, **101**
    sponging 96–7, **98**
    stencilling 97, **97**
    stippling **97**, 98–9
    verdigris **98**, 99–100
    woodgraining **100**, 100–1
panelling, timber *see* timber cladding
parlours, cottage **17**
parquet flooring 121, **121**
parsley 172
patchwork quilts 27
    making 136, **136**
pelargoniums 11, 89, **173**
Pennsylvania Dutch style 60
picture rails 41
pictures 74–5
    spattering technique for frames 102, **102**,
    103
pillowcases, adding lace to 132, **132**
pin cushion, making 132–3, **133**
pine:
    floorboards 121, **121**
    furniture 16, **33**, **195**
piping, disguising 46
plants 50–1, 150
    baskets for 74
    bathroom 89
    see also bulbs; flowers
plaster walls:
    Provençal treatment of **18**
    sealing 45
plastic-coated fabric **19**, 60, 129, **129**
plate racks **60**, 61
polish:
    beeswax 51
    lavender **177**
posies **150**, 162
pot pourris 174
    making 178–9, **180**
pots and pans 63
primulas **157**
Provençal style **18**–19
PVC-coated fabric **19**, 60, **64**, 129, **129**

quarry tiles 16, 59, **62**
quilts 55, **57**
    cleaning 55
    curtains from 16, **54**
    hanging as tapestry **56**
    'headboard' **57**
    as loose covers **54**, 72
    making patchwork 136, **136**
    patchwork 27
    as tablecloths 16, **54**, **57**, 136, **136**, **137**
quinces **171**

racks, overhead 63, 65
radiators 51–2, **52**
    disguising 52
    painting 52, **52**
ragging (painting technique) **64**, 97–8, **99**
Ranunculus **157**, **160**, **163**
rocking horses 85
rosemary 172, **172**, **173**
    sachets **173**
roses **155**
    candied 174
    crystallizing petals 174, **175**
    drying **162**, **174**
    skin lotion **175**
    see also pot pourris, making
rugs 14, 21, **22**, 71
    kelim **92**, **93**
    making from rags 69, 142, **142**
rush matting **36**, 48, 67, **73**

sachets, herb **173**
samplers:
    fabric 144, **144**
    needlework 27, **27**, 75
Santa Fé style 30–1
Satin Weave (Laura Ashley Collection) 131, **131**
savory 172, **172**
sconces, candle **20**, **69**, **75**
seagrass matting 48, 120, **120**
sealant, natural (for plaster walls) 45
Shakers, the 29
    boxes **28**, 29
    furniture 29, **29**, 48, **49**
    log basket **46**
sheds, storage systems for 199, **199**
sheets *see* bedlinen
shell collections 189, **189**
shelves **194**
    built-in 73
    kitchen 60–1, **61**, 195, **195**
shower curtains 87, 89
shutters 21, **21**, 26, 49, **49**
sideboards 67
sinks, kitchen 59, **60**
sisal matting 48, 120, **120**
sitting rooms *see* living rooms
skirtings:
    painted 22, 24, 26, 46

stripped **17**
    woodgraining 116, **116**
slate floors **119**
soap dishes 89
sofas 26, **26**, 71, **73**
    Biedermeier **44**
    fitted covers for **13**
    metal-framed **74**
soft furnishings 50
    cottage 16
    country-house 15
    fabrics for 128–31, **128–31**
    Mediterranean 22
    Santa Fé 30
    Shaker 29
    Swedish 25
    Tuscan 21
southernwood **173**
spattering (painting technique) 99, **101**
    on picture frame 102, **102**, **103**
spatterware 68
spongeware 68
sponging (painting technique) **64**, 68, 96–7
    lampbase 104, **104**, **105**
stencilling 27, 50, 97, **97**
    floorboards 27, 50
    wallpaper 27, 50, **51**, **60**, 83, **88**
    round windows **100**, 110, **110**
stippling **97**, 98–9
stone flooring **119**
    natural **119**
    Tuscan 21
stools 17
    padded 72
storage:
    containers 64, **196**, 197, **197**
    cupboards 59–60, **60**, 61, **61**, 62, **63**
    in garden sheds 199, **199**
    see also shelves
stoves 28, 51, 59, **62**
    kakelungen 25
swallowtail joints 28
Swedish style 24–5

tablecloths 68
    adding fringe to 134–5, **134–5**
    from bedspread 67
    Provençal 19, **19**
    quilts as 16, **54**, **57**, 136, **136**, **137**
    Swedish 25
    from tea towels 78
tables:
    bedside **78**, 79
    cane **189**

coffee 72–3
conservatory 93
cricket **92**
dining 29, **33**, 67, **69**
    displaying on 191, **191**
    from dough bin 71
    dressing 79
    Dutch **63**
    faux lacquering 114, **114**, **115**
    hall 91, **91**, 191
    kitchen 61
    pine **33**
    side 73
    three-legged (tripod) **17**, **73**, **92**
    see also centrepieces, table; tablecloths
televisions 34
tempera magra 21
terracotta pots 21
textiles see fabrics
    antique **72**
thyme 172, **172**
Ticking (Laura Ashley Collection) 131, **131**
ticking, loose covers from **13**
tiles:
    concrete 46, 48
    encaustic **119**
    fireplace 122, **122**, **123**
    floor **42**, **119**
    kitchen 59
    linoleum **118**
    marble **119**
    octagonal **119**
    Provençal 18
    quarry **16**, 59, **62**
    terracotta 18, **119**
    wall 59
timber cladding 16, **45**, 46, **59**, 75
tissue covers, making 132, **132**
toiletries, storing 87, 89, **89**
tongue-and-grooved cladding 16, **45**, 46
tool rack **199**
toothbrush holders 89
towels 50, 87
    rails for 87
toy chests 85
    trompe l'oeil 108, **108**, **109**
Traditional Cotton (Laura Ashley Collection)
    130–1, **130–1**
traveller's joy **150**, **157**
travertino marble 21
treen **191**
trompe l'oeil 108, **108**
trugs **183**
tulips 154, **154**, **161**
Tuscan rooms **20**, 21, **21**, **44**

upholstery fabrics 130–1, **130–1**

valances, bed 80
vegetable arrangements **149**, **158**
verdigris, imitation **98**, 99–100
    on chair 106, **106**, **107**
vinyl flooring 59, **62**
Voile 129, **129**

walls and wallcoverings:
    in children's rooms 83, **84**
    colourwashing 46, 96, **96**
    cottage 16
    country-house 14
    displays on 192, **192**
    dragging (painting technique) **96**, 98
    kitchen **45**, 59, **60**
    Mediterranean 22
    painting **20**, 21, 46
    Provençal 18, **18**
    ragging (painting technique) 97, **99**
    sealing newly plastered 45
    sealing paper in bathrooms 87
    spattering (painting technique) 99, **101**
    sponging (painting technique) 96–7, **98**
    stencilling 27, **60**, 50, **51**, 83, **88**, 97, **97**
    stippling (painting technique) **97**, 98–9
    striped **73**
    timber cladding for 16, **45**, 46, **59**, **75**
    Tuscan **20**, 21, **21**
    white **23**, 24, **41**, 41–2
wardrobes 79
washstand, Shaker **29**
whitewash 41–2
windows 11, 13, 15, 16, 24, 26
    disguising ugly view from 50
    hinged rails for **47**
    narrow 42
    non-matching 43
    short 42
    stencilling round 110, **110**, **111**
    see also curtains
window seats 72
Windsor chairs 26, **71**, **75**
wood: flooring 121, **121**
    wall cladding see timber cladding
woodgraining **100**, 100–1
    doors 116, **116**, **117**
work surfaces, kitchen 59
Woven Check (Laura Ashley Collection) 130, **130**
Woven Jacquard (Laura Ashley Collection) 131,
    131
wreaths:
    making 167, **167**, **171**
    see also garlands